HOW TO SELL COVERED CALLS

A Beginner's Guide to Renting Your Stocks for Monthly Income

MR. SINCERE

Sincere Books, LLC
Miami, Florida USA

How to Sell Covered Calls:
A Beginner's Guide to Renting Your
Stocks for Monthly Income

ISBN: 979-8-9923647-2-9 (trade paperback)
ISBN: 979-8-9923647-3-6 (ePub)
Also available for Kindle

Published by Sincere Books, LLC
http://www.michaelsincere.com

I dedicate this book to my amazing family,
who I love more than words can say.

Contents

Introduction

Thanks for taking the time to read my book! I am Mr. Sincere, a professional writer and teacher. In this book, I used my skills as an educator, investor, and trader to show a brilliant way to increase income and build wealth by renting stocks for monthly income.

How is it possible to build wealth using options? As I will describe, there is an easy-to-learn option strategy called *selling* (or *writing*) *covered calls* that makes it possible. The simplest way to understand the strategy is to think about it this way: It is similar to owning a house and renting it to a short-term tenant. When the lease expires, the house is rented again and again until the house is ultimately sold at a price of your choosing.

Writing (or selling) covered calls involves charging rent on stocks that you own while giving the "tenant" (i.e., renter) the right to buy those stocks. The more shares of stock owned, the greater the "rent money" received.

This strategy is ideal for investors who want to rent their stock(s) to speculators, and get paid for the opportunity. This strategy is one of the most basic option strategies to learn, and best of all, it comes with less risk compared to simply owning stocks.

When I speak about "risk," I am referring to the probability of losing money. Compared to other option strategies, selling or writing covered calls is "less risky," that is, it is still possible to lose money on a trade, but the probability of losing is less when compared to owning stock or using speculative option strategies.

In return for less danger, the payout may not be as large when compared to using more speculative strategies.

Therefore, if you're a person who wants to make big money quickly by speculating with options, this book may not meet your needs. Selling covered calls is for patient, longer-term investors who want to earn money by selling call options on stocks that they already own. You will not make an immediate fortune with this strategy, but you can make a decent sum of money periodically (perhaps monthly or every few weeks) for as long as you continue to sell covered calls.

For many beginners, writing (or selling) covered calls is the ONLY options strategy they need to learn. I have personally tried nearly every option strategy imaginable, and I can confidently say that selling covered calls is my favorite because it provides income while letting me sleep at night (and not worry I will lose all my money).

I wrote this book to show you how to receive monthly income while reducing the possibility of losing money. If I can teach you how to do that, then I consider my book a success.

Who is this book for?

This book is for:

- Anyone who wants to earn a few hundred or a few thousand dollars every month with stocks they already own
- Beginners who are curious about options but don't know how to get started

- Those with small or large investment accounts
- Traders who were unsuccessful with other option strategies
- Beginners who want to learn about selling covered calls without wading through long-winded explanations, confusing vocabulary, complicated charts, or strategies that require a PhD to understand.

You learn:

- How to sell covered calls for steady income
- How to reduce investment anxiety
- How to choose stocks that generate income for months and years
- How to analyze an *option chain* so you can receive a reasonable return on your investment without taking large risks
- How to avoid unexpected traps that snare many novice option traders
- Ways to reduce risk

START WITH THE BASICS

I'll begin this book by introducing you to the options market, where you will learn about selling covered calls. This strategy is easy to use to generate instant cash. The first two chapters are the most important as you learn the rules and terminology. You will also learn that stocks and options work together like a well-oiled machine.

Although writing covered calls is a relatively simple, lower-risk options strategy, it requires time to understand. Too many beginners skip over the covered call strategy to jump into more exciting and speculative strategies. Many of these option strategies have sexy names that promise fantastic returns—but some are extremely risky. You are wise to learn about selling covered calls before jumping into more exotic strategies (if you ever do).

I have spoken with a few readers of option books who told me that it took them *years* to understand some books about options. After hearing that, I did my best to make sure that it would not take you a long time to learn the simple strategy of selling covered calls.

This is important: You do not need to know everything about options to use them to make money. That really would take years. I say this more than once, but for most investors, the only options strategy they need to learn is writing covered calls.

In fact, my goal is to get you started within a short time period. For those who want to learn about this fascinating strategy, you should enjoy this book. I made sure I gave you all of the information needed while still keeping you interested. That is what all good teachers do!

> If you want to learn about other option strategies, I strongly recommend a best-selling book, *Understanding Options* (McGraw Hill), which has sold over 100,000 copies. (Hint: I wrote it).

SELL COVERED CALLS FOR INCOME

One of the best reasons to sell covered calls is that you can make money every month or quarter. This is a way of increasing *cash flow*, one of the smartest ways to generate additional income from the stocks you own.

This strategy is popular with many risk-adverse investors because they know exactly how much income they'll receive. Another great reason to sell covered calls is that you don't need a fortune to make money. As you'll learn, the more shares of stock you own, the more money you can make.

Selling covered calls boosts investment returns, especially during a sideways or gently rising market. While many investors are waiting for their stocks to make a move higher, you are collecting money.

IS SELLING COVERED CALLS TOO GOOD TO BE TRUE?

When first hearing about selling covered calls, it almost sounds too good to be true. Imagine this: Investors get paid while holding a stock. As mentioned several times, they are acting as a landlord who rents stock to option speculators. The speculators give them money (i.e., *premium*), which is immediately placed into their account.

Selling call options on stocks is an uncomplicated, straightforward way to bring in income. It's not as unpredictable as many other strategies and if the right stock is chosen, it can generate steady income every week, month, or every few months.

I know many people who do this. For example, a call options seller I knew, the late Warren Kaplan, had been writing covered calls for over 40 years. This strategy allowed him to build a sizeable fortune. Here's the part that really surprised me: Kaplan only sold a few call options at a time.

One of his strategies was to buy a few shares of stock, perhaps 25 or 50 shares at one time. Eventually, when he owned a stock position of at least 100 shares, he sold 1 covered call.

By buying shares slowly, he got a chance to observe how the stock price behaved. When he was comfortable owning the stock, he continued accumulating shares. It goes to show that an investor doesn't need a fortune to make money with this strategy.

To answer the question above, although covered call writing is an excellent strategy, it is *not* too good to be true. You will learn later that unlike more speculative option strategies, you may make less money using this strategy in return for reduced risk. (I explain these concepts in more detail in later chapters.)

Are options too risky?

Is this strategy risk-free? No. There is no such thing as a risk-free investment because all investments involve some risk. But compared to other option strategies that come with huge risks, selling covered calls is suitable for most investors. It is designed to increase cash flow while boosting income by compounding the rent money as well as dividends.

Many people believe that using options is a "get-rich casino" that is more like gambling than investing. Other people are intimidated by options or have heard the horror stories (primarily because traders used complex option strategies that are not for beginners).

Fortunately, I steer you away from the treacherous strategies and focus on the less-complicated covered call strategy. As you will learn, when selling covered calls, you are not gambling, and the dangers are minimal compared to owning stocks.

Therefore, if anyone tells you that *all* option strategies are too risky or confusing, tell them it's not true. Only the most speculative option strategies are risky and confusing. Selling covered calls is not speculative and the risks are manageable.

Bottom line: Selling covered calls is a very comfortable place to begin your options journey.

WHAT IF YOU DON'T HAVE MUCH MONEY?

Many beginners get lured into more speculative strategies because of the low cost. For example, they could be tempted to trade penny stocks, or buy options that seek a huge return on their investment (ROI). Fortunately, you can make a good return by selling covered calls with a modest sum. Later in the book, I show you how.

Bottom line: Yes, you can sell covered calls on stocks even if you don't have much money.

LET'S BEGIN!

Are you ready to get started? Great! Because I'm ready to teach you how to use options to build wealth without taking big chances. I'm excited to be able to teach you about this option strategy, one that I use myself.

I tried to make this book the most useful you ever read. If I'm successful, you'll be able to use options to make money indefinitely—and without too much risk. Once again, I didn't say there was no risk, only that the risk is less than with other option strategies.

And now, let's begin learning about selling covered calls. I hope you find it as fascinating as I did when I first began selling them years ago.

Note: As a former teacher, I have a habit of repeating information, which helps to reinforce what you already learned. If you have an excellent memory or read the book from start to finish, this may be annoying, and I apologize. If your memory is less than perfect, or if you read only a few chapters at a time, you should appreciate the repetition (at least I hope so!).

Chapter 1

Option Basics

In this important chapter, I'll introduce you to the world of options. I'll begin with a brief overview, and later dig deeper into the covered call strategy. I'll also introduce important vocabulary words that help give you a strong options foundation.

As I said in the introduction, before selling covered calls, you must already own a stock. In fact, the whole idea of this strategy is to sell covered calls on stocks that you already own. In a way, you are renting the stocks you own to option speculators. They are willing to pay money (*premium*) for the *right* to take possession of your stock.

The goal of this popular strategy is to generate extra income or cash flow by selling (or writing) the call option to option buyers (i.e., speculators or hedgers).

If you're still not exactly sure how this strategy works, or the rules, don't worry because you will understand as you continue reading. Learning how to sell covered calls is similar to learning a new language, so be patient.

The Options Contract

The first thing you should know about options is that they are *contracts*. Just the word, "contract," makes some people nervous. Even though an option is technically a legal contract, you don't need a lawyer to buy or sell them. Most important, the terms of the contract are pretty basic.

Stock options are contracts that give the option owner the *right* to buy or sell stock. I emphasize the word, "right," because options give choices to their owners. (Hint: This is the reason why they are called "options.")

The interesting part about an options contract, one that is very important, is that an option is linked to an *underlying stock*. According to the rules, to use the covered call strategy, you must own at least 100 shares of stock (i.e., the *underlying stock*). Once you own at least 100 shares of stock, you are allowed to sell 1 covered call. (If you own 200 shares of stock, you can sell 2 covered calls, and so on.)

There is another vocabulary word I want to explain. Some of you may wonder why the strategy is called selling *covered* calls. The word, "covered," simply means that you own the stock and, if required to do so, can deliver the shares to the option owner.

If you didn't own the stock, you'd be trading "naked," or "uncovered." Selling *naked* in the options market is extremely risky because losses are theoretically unlimited when selling calls on stocks that you do not own. Being a covered call seller eliminates that possibility.

Why Sell Covered Calls

I briefly discussed in the introduction the reasons someone may want to sell covered calls. In case you didn't read it or remember what I wrote, there are two main reasons to use this strategy:

1. Receive premium: When selling covered calls, you collect income (also referred to as *premium*), the main reason for using this strategy. The great thing about selling covered calls is you receive the premium upfront, right at the beginning. Therefore, you can use a stock you own to generate cash flow, month after month (or whatever time frame you like). Many people believe that selling covered calls is one of the most brilliant ways to use the options market, and for less risk than with most other option strategies.

2. Use the options market to sell your stocks: Many stock owners don't realize that a clever way to sell a stock they own is to use the options market. Briefly, after deciding to sell one of your stocks, begin by selling covered calls. You receive a little extra income and the stock is (hopefully) sold at a price you specify. I show how this works in more detail in Chapter 4.

Bottom line: The goal of this strategy is to use your stocks to generate income. This is the beauty of selling call options and why this strategy is so popular with millions of people who sell call options to boost their income and bring in monthly or quarterly cash.

The rest of this chapter is devoted to teaching you the unique language of the options market. Once you understand the following terms, you'll be ready to sell your first covered call.

THE OPTIONS VOCABULARY

Before we go any further, I should caution you that if this is the first time you have been introduced to options, the vocabulary introduced below may seem like "Greek" to you. At first, it may seem like you are learning a new language, and in fact, you are. Later, when you look at real-life examples, and after making your first options trade, it will be much easier.

Let's begin with the basics, and that is learning about the differences between *calls* and *puts*.

1. **Calls and Puts**

   There are only two types of options: a *call* and a *put*. With these two types of options, the option buyer can take only two actions: *buy* or *sell*. Although many people try to dazzle you with dozens of fancy-sounding option names and strategies, all option trades are based on buying and selling calls and puts.

   Buying a *call option* is similar to "going long" a stock (it means someone believes the underlying stock price will rise). Buying a *put option* is similar to "going short" a stock (it means someone believes the stock price will fall). Buying calls and puts are speculative strategies. Fortunately, selling covered calls is considered a lower-risk, conservative options strategy.

   Here is the important part: When you *sell* covered calls, you want the underlying stock to either stay at the same price or rise slightly in value. This will make a lot more sense when we actually start selling calls in Chapter 4.

2. **Underlying stock**

   I introduced this term a few times in the book because it's so important. Before you can sell a covered call, you must first own an *underlying stock*.

An option is simply a contract that gives the option owner the right to buy or sell 100 shares of a specified stock at a predetermined price for a limited time. In this book, we use options to sell the underlying stock to the option buyer.

Note: Another term for option is "derivatives," which means that the value of an option contract is derived from another financial product. In this book, that financial product is 100 shares of stock. Therefore, the option contract is derived from or linked to the value of the underlying stock.

I can't stress enough how important it is to choose a suitable underlying stock. I discuss how to do this in Chapter 3.

Review

As you know, this book is devoted to only one strategy: selling covered calls. As you may remember, the term, "covered," simply means that you own the underlying stock. If you didn't own the underlying stock, options people would say that you are "selling naked," or selling uncovered options.

3. Simple options formula

If you're worried by the word, "formula," don't be. The following formula is easy to understand. You already know that an options contract and stock are linked. This simple formula shows you exactly how:

1 option contract = 100 shares of stock

To be specific, 1 call option represents the *right* to buy 100 shares. Therefore, 3 option contracts give their owner the right to buy 300 shares of the underlying stock, and 5 option contracts = 500 shares of stock.

Note: After you have made your first option trade, all of these isolated pieces of information will make a lot more sense.

4. Premium

I mentioned *premium* several times. Premium is the total amount received when you sell one covered call option. The premium is very important to covered call sellers. Obviously, before selling any covered call, you will look up how much money, or premium, you can collect.

If the premium is high enough to meet your financial goals, you will likely proceed with the trade. If the amount is too small, you may want to look for another trade, perhaps one that provides a higher cash flow.

Those are all the vocabulary words for now. In Chapter 2, when you learn about the *option chain*, I will introduce several more important words such as the *strike price*, *expiration date*, and *bid price*. As you will see, it's exciting because you can choose among many different strike prices, expiration dates, and bid prices.

Before moving to the next chapter, if you are unfamiliar with the stock market, the following sidebar should be helpful. (However, if you know a lot about the stock market, feel free to skip the sidebar.)

If you don't know much about the stock market

It's important to have a basic knowledge of the stock market before selling covered calls. Fortunately, the stock market is pretty straightforward: your three main choices are to buy, sell, or hold.

The stock market is a marketplace or auction where companies initially list shares of stock so they can raise money for their corporation.

To buy and sell shares of stock, and potentially make money with stocks or options, you must sign up with a brokerage firm.

The brokerage firm

A brokerage firm is a company licensed to buy and sell stocks on the stock exchange on behalf of their clients, which is you and me. If you want to sell covered calls, you must open a brokerage account. That allows you to trade stocks. Opening a brokerage account is as easy as opening a checking or savings account. You can open it online or visit the brokerage firm (if it is brick-and-mortar).

Buying stocks

When you buy stocks, you "share" in the profits (which is why stock investors are also called "shareholders.") The only reason to buy stocks in companies is to make money. The shareholder earns money when the stock price moves higher. You lose money when the stock price moves lower.

To make money in the stock market, it's important to own stocks in corporations that are selling a lot of goods and services, and are making decent profits. I'm sure you can think of a lot of successful companies with products that you buy, stores that you visit, and items that you use every day.

Think of successful stocks such as Apple, Home Depot, Amazon, Lowe's, Disney, Nike, Microsoft, Alphabet, Costco, Walmart, Nvidia, Meta, to name a few. These are just some of the thousands of stocks you can buy.

The great news about investing in stocks is you don't need a lot of money to get started. In fact, you can open a brokerage account with no initial deposit, and then add to it later.

Permission to trade options

When you're ready to sell covered calls, you must ask the brokerage for permission to trade options. The good news is it's easy to get permission to sell covered calls. (After you read this book, you will have no problem getting permission.) Note: The specific steps to apply for an options account are discussed in Chapter 9.

Note: To learn much more about stocks and the stock market, I recommend two books, *Understanding Stocks* (McGraw Hill), and *Help Your Child Build Wealth* (Wiley), both written by me.

If these two books don't meet your needs, there are tons of other books about the stock market available online or at the bookstore.

CONCLUSION

I hope you are eager to continue as I teach you how to sell covered calls. I know that it takes a lot of motivation to keep reading. As I said in the introduction, learning about options is similar to learning another language. Please keep reading!

In Chapter 2, you'll learn how to read the *option chain*, the road map that everyone who uses options must learn. It's not hard to understand and if the option chain is used properly, it will be very helpful when it comes to choosing which specific options to sell.

CHAPTER 2

THE OPTION CHAIN

This chapter is where I introduce the *option chain,* typically one of the first option screens you'll look at on the broker's website before making any trade, including selling a covered call.

Together, we will analyze the different parts of the option chain. After reading this chapter and studying a few examples, the option chain should become your friend.

INTRODUCING THE OPTION CHAIN

Since a picture is worth a thousand words, below are two option chains for the underlying stock, Coca-Cola (KO), when it was trading at $65.78 per share on October 29 (but it's guaranteed to be selling at a different price when you read this).

Note that the expiration date of November 29 was one month away from the example date. Important: The following examples are not trade recommendations.

COCA-COLA AT $65.78 PER SHARE AND A NOVEMBER 29TH EXPIRATION DATE

65.78 -0.88 (-1.33%)

As of 1:42 PM EDT. Market Open.

Nov 29, 2024 ⌄ All Strike Prices ⌄ List ⌄ Calls ⌄

Calls

Contract Name	Last Trade Date (EDT)	Strike	Last Price	Bid	Ask
KO241129C00060000	10/21/2024 5:44 PM	60	10.04	5.60	6.25
KO241129C00061000	10/29/2024 4:47 PM	61	5.10	4.90	5.30
KO241129C00062000	10/16/2024 1:38 PM	62	8.60	4.15	4.30
KO241129C00063000	10/24/2024 1:55 PM	63	5.10	3.30	3.40
KO241129C00064000	10/25/2024 7:49 PM	64	3.45	2.17	2.76
KO241129C00065000	10/29/2024 2:17 PM	65	1.85	1.75	1.81
KO241129C00066000	10/29/2024 2:34 PM	66	1.32	1.15	1.22
KO241129C00067000	10/29/2024 4:07 PM	67	0.70	0.68	0.73
KO241129C00068000	10/29/2024 5:03 PM	68	0.40	0.37	0.42
KO241129C00069000	10/29/2024 4:49 PM	69	0.19	0.19	0.22

Figure 2.1 Coca-Cola Option Chain
Source: Yahoo Finance

The following pieces of information on the option chain are the most important:

- *Expiration date* (November 29 in this example)
- *Strike price* (ranging from 60 to 69 in this example)
- *Bid price* (ranging from a low of $0.19 per share to a high of $5.60 in this example)
- *Bid-ask spread:* The difference between the bid and ask prices

Once you decipher the option chain vocabulary, it's easy to sell covered calls. Let's take a closer look.

THE EXPIRATION DATE, BID AND ASK PRICE, AND STRIKE PRICE

Consider the option chain as a road map. All option traders must study it closely before placing a trade. The option chain contains a series of *expiration dates*, a range of *strike prices*, and a list of *bid and ask prices*.

THE OPTION CONTRACT

If you look at Figure 2.1, on the left side of the option chain, you see a long list of letters and numbers, starting with KO in this example. That long name describes the specific option contract symbol. Don't worry! You don't have to memorize it or study it.

In fact, you don't have to pay attention to the contract name at all since all of the information about the contract will appear on your trade screen. The purpose of that long name is to allow the computer to sort option contracts.

> Note: For those who are interested, the long quote, KO241129C00065000 tells you this: KO is the symbol of the underlying stock, in this example, it refers to Coca Cola. 24-11-29 is the November 29, 2024 expiration date. C stands for call (or P for put). 65 is the strike price (which ranges from 60 to 69 in Figure 2.1. You will learn much more about strike prices in this chapter.

THE EXPIRATION DATE

If you look at the two option chains in Figure 2.1 and Figure 2.2 (below), you will notice that the expiration dates are different. In Figure 2.1, the expiration date is November 29. In Figure 2.2, the expiration date is December 20.

> Note: Your brokerage screen may look different than what you see above. You may see a long list of expiration dates ranging from a few days (from the trade date) to next week, next month, and many more months afterwards.

When selling a covered call, the expiration date is part of the contract, so you must select a date. Typically, covered call sellers choose an expiration date that is 30- to 45-days from the current day, but that depends on a variety of personal factors such as how much premium they want to receive, and the price target they have for the underlying stock.

Right now, we will choose an expiration date that is approximately a month away. That is a common time frame for many covered call sellers. As you gain more experience, you may decide that shorter or more distant expiration dates suit your needs better.

The current date at this writing is October 29. That means you may want to choose a late-November or December expiration date, one that is approximately one or two months away.

Note: Some covered call sellers choose extremely short expiration dates such as one or two weeks. However, if selling covered calls is new to you, stick with a 30- to 45-day expiration date because it offers more time for the trade to be profitable. You can choose shorter or longer time periods in the future.

Here's an important clue: Below, you will learn about *bid prices*, which helps determine how much premium you'll receive. That's when you'll learn that the farther away the expiration date, the higher the premium you'll receive. And the shorter the date, the lower the premium you'll collect. This will be explained in more detail later in this chapter, so don't worry about why this is true.

To help visualize how the bid price changes as the expiration date changes, below is the option chain for KO for a two-month expiration date (i.e., December 20). Note that the farther out the expiration date, the higher the bid price, and the higher the premium received.

Note: The following examples are not trade recommendations.

COCA-COLA AT $65.78 PER SHARE WITH A DECEMBER 20TH EXPIRATION DATE

65.78 -0.88 (-1.33%)

As of 1:42 PM EDT. Market Open.

Dec 20, 2024 ⌄ All Strike Prices ⌄ List ⌄ Calls ⌄

Calls

Contract Name	Last Trade Date (EDT)	Strike	Last Price	Bid	Ask
KO241220C00037500	4/22/2024 4:21 PM	37.5	23.09	23.60	27.55
KO241220C00040000	9/12/2024 7:14 PM	40	31.45	28.10	31.00
KO241220C00047500	10/23/2024 3:01 PM	47.5	20.40	18.50	18.60
KO241220C00050000	10/16/2024 4:47 PM	50	20.89	16.00	16.85
KO241220C00052500	9/12/2024 2:16 PM	52.5	18.75	17.35	18.25
KO241220C00055000	10/28/2024 4:34 PM	55	11.90	11.00	11.15
KO241220C00057500	10/29/2024 2:57 PM	57.5	8.85	8.55	8.70
KO241220C00060000	10/29/2024 4:32 PM	60	6.21	6.15	6.25
KO241220C00062500	10/29/2024 3:57 PM	62.5	3.95	3.85	4.00
KO241220C00065000	10/29/2024 5:00 PM	65	2.07	2.05	2.09
KO241220C00067500	10/29/2024 5:15 PM	67.5	0.83	0.80	0.82
KO241220C00070000	10/29/2024 5:11 PM	70	0.26	0.25	0.28

Figure 2.2 Coca-Cola Option Chain
Source: Yahoo Finance

When you compare the November 29 option chain with the December 20 option chain, you see that the bid prices are higher for the later date. That is because the longer the expiration date, the more premium you'll receive.

As mentioned earlier, it also means that your stock is tied up for a lot longer. Choosing an expiration date is an important decision. These are the kind of choices that covered call sellers must make every day. You weigh the amount of premium you may collect with how long your stock will be controlled by the buyer.

To repeat what I wrote earlier, for many covered call sellers, a 30- to 45-day expiration date is a popular choice, but everyone has different goals, so in the end, you have to make your own decision which expiration date is best.

The Strike Price

Another important aspect of the option contract is the *strike price* (probably the most important). The strike price is a fixed price at which you may be required to sell the underlying stock. To be more specific, it's the price at which the option can be *exercised* (discussed in detail later). In fact, some traders refer to the strike price as the "exercise price."

In Figure 2.1 and Figure 2.2, you see a list of *strike prices* in the strike price column.

A Very Important Number

By itself, the strike price is just a number. In fact, when selling covered calls, you always have a choice of several strike prices. Strike prices range from $5 with no upper limit because they are always based on the price of the underlying stock.

Therefore, a 66 strike means that you, the shareholder, is granting the call owner the right to buy 100 shares of KO at $66 per share at anytime before the option expires. It also means you are obligated to *sell* KO at $66 per share on the expiration date, but only if the option buyer "calls the stock away." (We will discuss this action later.)

Selling a call with a 67 strike price means you may become obligated to sell KO at $67 per share on or before the expiration date (November 29 in Figure 2.1). Another example: Choosing the 68 strike means you may become obligated to sell KO for $68 per share on or before the expiration date (November 29 in Figure 2.1).

NOBODY'S PERFECT

You will soon learn that there is no way to choose the perfect strike price. It is as much art as science, and each trader has their own reasons for choosing a specific option to sell. The strike price is an important factor in determining the premium. The goal for most people is to choose a strike price that gives them a decent premium, which varies for each person.

> Hint: In Figure 2.1, there are many strike price choices, but one appropriate choice is the 67 strike, which is 1.22 points higher than KO's current price of $65.78 per share. That gives a premium of $.68 per share.

Note: A covered call seller may also choose a strike price that is *below* the current stock price. This may seem to be a strange idea, but I'll explain it more thoroughly in Chapter 4.

Perhaps another trading example may help you better understand how to decide on a strike price.

Strike price (Review)

Let's say you own a stock that is currently selling for $35 per share. You decide to sell covered calls on those shares so you can receive monthly income.

Once you make that decision, you look at a range of strike prices and pick one. For example, you may see a 33, 34, 35, 36, 37, 38, and 39.

Here's the important part: Let's say you choose to sell a covered call on your stock at the 37 strike. This means that you may become obligated to sell this stock for $37 per share on or before the expiration date. That is two points higher than its current price.

Bid price

If you look at Figure 2.1 above, you will see a *bid* column and an *ask* column. Because we are selling covered calls, the column we care most about is the BID column. This is the current highest published price (i.e., premium) that a buyer is willing to pay for the call.

1. *Premium*: the cash you receive when selling one call option
2. *Bid price*: the amount a buyer is willing to pay for the call

Basic math

Calculating the premium is simple math. When you sell the call option for $.80, it means that you receive $80. That sum is deposited into your account and you will see it on the next business day.

Here's the math: $.80 premium x 100 (or 1 contract, representing 100 shares of stock) = $80.

Here's an analogy I've used several times: Basically, you rent your stock to an option buyer and will receive $80 as the premium (or rent money, as if you were a landlord). You still own the stock but the option buyer has complete control over those 100 shares.

In fact, you are not allowed to sell those shares until the option buyer decides whether to buy the stock (*exercise* their option) at the strike price. That is the option buyer's decision, and you have no say in the matter. However, you get to keep the premium ($80 in this example) plus any dividends. Note: Fortunately, there is a way to close the position early, which will be discussed in Chapter 6.

All you did was lend your stock to a call option buyer until the expiration date (technically, you loaned the *rights* to buy your stock). On the expiration date, the random option buyer may take one of three actions:

1. Buy your stock at the strike price. This eliminates the position and provides a successful outcome for the trade.
2. Do nothing, allowing the option to expire and become worthless.
3. Sell the option in the market place.

One thing remains true: No matter which choice is made, the premium is yours to keep.

IF YOU OWNED 500 SHARES OF STOCK

Let's say you owned 500 shares of stock and wanted to sell 5 covered calls at the $.80 bid price. By selling 5 call option contracts, you receive $400 in premium (500 shares x $.80).

The whole purpose of selling covered calls is to receive a reasonable premium from stocks you own. That means choosing a strike price that gives you the best "bang for your buck." To achieve that goal, you must take the time to study and understand the option chain.

THE IMPORTANCE OF RETURN ON INVESTMENT (ROI)

When thinking about premium size, don't only think of it in dollar (or other currency) terms, but in ROI terms. For example, if a stock is trading for $20 per share and you receive an $80 premium, that's a 4% return on the $2,000 investment in one month. In this example, an $80 premium is very high. However, if a stock were priced at $400 per share, the $80 premium would provide only .20 percent, a very dismal return.

With experience, you will see which expiration dates, strike prices, and premiums offer the biggest reward. This is what you want: a solid return on your investment coupled with acceptable risk.

If you are first learning this strategy, your objective is to learn HOW to sell covered calls, including how to make strategic decisions such as choosing an appropriate call option.

WHICH IS THE IDEAL EXPIRATION DATE?

Unfortunately, there is no ideal expiration date. Many decisions go into choosing the date. For example, earnings announcements, stock market volatility, whether you prefer to sell shorter- or longer-term options, and if you have the patience to sit and wait for the expiration date to arrive.

When you use the options market as a way to sell stock, then a shorter expiration date may be appropriate. The downside to a shorter expiration is that the premium will be smaller (longer expiration options come with higher premiums). However, ROI is likely to be higher for short-term options.

Warning: Before choosing an expiration date, be aware of scheduled earnings announcements or other newsworthy events that could affect the price of the underlying stock.

Important fact: When choosing an expiration date, the stock is controlled by the option buyer until the market closes for trading on that date. In other words, your stock is “tied up” until the option expires. The option buyer is willing to pay a premium for the right to be in control of your stock until the expiration date.

Quiz: Which expiration date is best?

As you may remember, the later the expiration month, the greater the premium. Nevertheless, for a variety of reasons, it may not be a wise move to choose a later expiration month. For example, in Figure 2.1, the bid price of the KO November 29 expiration date with a 67 strike is $.68. In Figure 2.2, the bid price of the KO December 20 expiration date with a 67.50 strike is $.80.

Question: Which expiration date should you choose—the November 29 with a $.68 bid price and $68 premium or the December 20 with an $.80 bid price and an $80 premium?

Answer: If you can collect $68 for a one-month call option, is it really worth your while to extend the life of the option contract for another month for a measly extra $12? Not in my opinion. Thus, the November 29 expiration date with a $68 premium makes the most sense in this example. These are the kind of decisions covered call writers have to make with every transaction.

TIME IS YOUR FRIEND

Here is the good news for call option sellers such as yourself: Instead of time being your enemy, time is your friend. Unlike stocks, which exist forever (unless a company merges or goes out of business), option contracts expire. This is good for option sellers but not for option buyers, who are always concerned that time will run out before they make the money they hoped for. "Time decay" is the enemy of option buyers (but a friend to option sellers).

Option buyers constantly have to monitor their option positions. Not so with call option sellers: They should occasionally monitor their position, but they don't have to watch it all of the time like option buyers do.

TWO SCENARIOS AT EXPIRATION

The passing of time is a good thing for covered call sellers. When time runs out, either of the two scenarios may occur, and both are positive for the call option seller. Either the stock is *called away* (i.e., sold at the strike price), or it's not called away. Either way, you keep the premium. Both situations benefit the covered call seller.

Remember that when you sold the call option, you were willing to sell the stock, so if it is "called away" at the strike price, it is not something to regret. Your strategy worked.

CONCLUSION

Congratulations! The first two chapters were the meat of the covered call strategy, and the most challenging (if you are new to options). The rest of the book should be relatively easy. Soon, you'll study covered call examples using the terminology just learned.

As you probably know, it takes skill to choose a desirable strike price, underlying stock, and expiration date. Although the covered call strategy is one of the easiest to learn and understand, it's still not as easy as many people think.

In Chapter 3, you will discover that one of the keys to success is choosing a suitable underlying stock. In this chapter, you will learn how to find underlying stocks that have good future prospects (although there are never any guarantees).

CHAPTER 3

HOW TO FIND SUITABLE UNDERLYING STOCKS

One of the most important decisions you make when selling covered calls is choosing an underlying stock that helps generate decent profits. With the covered call strategy, you're not looking at making "a killing." The goal is to bring in good-sized profits without taking too much risk. Choosing a good underlying stock is one of your keys to success when using this strategy.

Therefore, a fitting underlying stock is one that has moved slightly higher in the recent past, and you believe may do so in the future. To achieve better results and higher premium, you may want to look for what I call "Steady Freddie" stocks, or stocks that come with a little more volatility.

Because these stocks may move slightly higher for months or years, buying such stocks may be a profitable venture (with no guarantees). Steady Freddie stocks can generate consistent profits year after year, especially when they never quite rise to the option's strike price.

These stocks serve a dual purpose: they are excellent buy-and-hold stocks, and they may be good candidates for the covered call strategy. The good news is there are hundreds of stocks that fit the "Steady Freddie" profile—if you take time to look. I will help you do that in this chapter.

CHARACTERISTICS OF APPROPRIATE UNDERLYING STOCKS

Many covered call sellers don't know that a major key to success is finding the right underlying stock. In fact, no matter which option strategy you adopt, choosing a suitable underlying stock is important.

Many speculators have it reversed: they believe that to make money, they must find the right option, similar to discovering a winning lottery ticket. In reality, the path to success is finding an appropriate underlying stock with a decent-priced option to sell. The combination of these two features often leads to a successful trade.

Fortunately, there are thousands of stocks you can choose from, but let's zero in on a few stocks that may bring in good profits for months and years into the future.

What underlying stocks are ideal covered call candidates? A few of the stocks that have fit this criterion in the past include Coca-Cola, AT&T, IBM, Microsoft, Walmart, Home Depot, Lowe's, to name a few. Also, many stocks that are included in the Dow Jones Industrial Average or the S&P 500 are probably great choices for this strategy. It is a good place to start your search.

Caveat: Although many of these stocks performed well in the past, there is no guarantee they will do so in the future. As time passes, some winning stocks may fall out of favor and be replaced with even better-performing stocks.

Let's explore a few of the specific characteristics of underlying stocks to look for when selling covered calls.

1. Stocks that pay small dividends

   Desirable stocks may be large-cap, blue-chip stocks (although they don't have to be). Sometimes, these stocks pay dividends, which means the company's board of directors give back some of the profits to shareholders. Although not always true, stocks that pay dividends may be good covered call candidates, as long as the option premium provides an acceptable return on investment (ROI).

   It's true that a number of covered call sellers seek out stocks that pay dividends. Although this is not a bad idea, when a dividend-paying stock is not very volatile, then its options may trade with small premiums. That is why stocks that pay small dividends are often attractive as covered call candidates (assuming the return on investment meets the call writer's expectations).

2. Moderate volatility

   As mentioned earlier, covered call sellers want stocks that are not too volatile but also not boring. Stocks with some volatility have higher premiums, which is good for covered call sellers. Stocks with too much volatility, however, while tempting because the premiums can be quite high, may be too risky for covered call sellers. Covered call sellers don't like surprises, one reason why "hot" technology stocks mentioned in the media or online should be avoided.

3. Liquid stocks with a lot of volume

The stocks that many covered call sellers like often have high liquidity and high daily volume. When a stock is liquid, it means it's easy to buy and sell the shares. Therefore, choose stocks that are higher than $10 per share.

Note: Low-priced stocks should be avoided, especially those under $5 per share. Not only will the premium be small, but these stocks are often too volatile.

4. Stocks that are above their *moving averages*

   Stocks that are above their 20-day, 50-day, and 100-day *moving averages* on a three-month time frame are often good candidates for the covered call strategy. Conversely, stocks that fall well below their moving averages may not ideal candidates for this strategy. (An explanation of moving averages is in the sidebar below.)

In theory, if you chose an underlying stock that fits the guidelines above, your stock has a decent chance of behaving well, not just for weeks, but for years. However, as we all know, the stock market is unpredictable. That means even the best stocks can fall out of favor and move lower in the future.

Moving averages

Moving averages are technical indicators displayed on a chart that show the average value of a security's closing price over a specific time period, such as the last 20, 50, 100, or 200 days. Laying the moving average on top of a stock or index helps identify market direction. Pull up any stock chart to see two or three multi-colored moving average lines displayed. Stocks that are above the moving average lines are trending higher. Stocks below the moving average lines are trending lower.

When the underlying stock falls below one or more of these important moving averages, it is time to reconsider holding the stock. However, if your stock is solid with good prospects for the future based on fundamental analysis (i.e., good earnings, pays dividends, solid balance sheet, and little debt), then there is no reason to sell in a panic, especially if you want to gamble on the decline being only a temporary pullback.

You can find moving averages on a three-month time frame by pulling up a stock chart on your broker's website, or at numerous online financial websites. You can also learn more about moving averages by reading my book, *Understanding Stocks* (McGraw Hill).

Underlying Stocks That Are Poor Choices

I spent most of this chapter telling you which stocks are best for selling covered calls. It may be helpful to learn about stocks that could be poor candidates for selling covered calls.

The following are my suggestions for characteristics of underlying stocks to avoid when selling covered calls.

These are guidelines and not rules, meaning there are exceptions.

1. Volatile stocks that make huge daily price moves

   As mentioned earlier, underlying stocks that are too volatile are typically not ideal candidates for the covered call strategy. These stocks, often in the technology sector, may be good for short-term traders, but not for covered call sellers.

   Admittedly, it may be tempting for covered call sellers to choose volatile stocks because the premium is often quite high. Nevertheless, don't get fooled into buying wild stocks just because of their high premium.

   If you like to own these volatile stocks and if you want them to be a regular part of your stock portfolio, then by all means, continue to make such investments. Plus, if you are willing to sell covered calls and establish a limit for the potential profit, then these companies may make great covered call stocks. Again, don't buy these stocks just because the premiums are so high.

   For example, a stock like Google or Nvidia may be wonderful stocks to own if you can handle the stomach-churning plunges and rallies, sometimes within one day! Although the premiums are often rich, the downside risk is too great, especially when the technology sector gets hit.

   For example, if the stock drops by too much, although you keep that rich premium, you lose money as the stock keeps falling. That's why you may want to avoid selling calls on stocks that behave erratically.

In addition, if a stock you want to buy is exploding higher, although you make a profit, you'll miss out on any gains past the strike price. In fact, all profits above the strike price belongs to the call option buyer, not to the call option seller. In this example, it would be better if you held the stock without selling covered calls, no matter how high the option premium.

2. Low-priced stocks under $10

As mentioned earlier, stocks that are selling for less than $5 or $10 per share are usually not good candidates for the covered call strategy. The premium on these low-priced stocks are so small that it's not worth your time to buy them.

Typically, these stocks are low-priced for a reason, and it's usually because the company is not making money, or worse, it's a scam. Research suggests that most people lose money buying the "pennies," or stocks selling for less than $5 per share.

Some people are attracted to low-priced stocks because they can buy more shares, which allows them to sell more covered calls. However, many times these low-priced, low-volume stocks backfire on the investor by going out of business or not providing enough premium.

3. Stocks that are moving lower (i.e., they are losers)

Stocks that are consistently moving lower should usually be avoided by nearly everyone, including covered call sellers. For many people, it's common sense to not buy stocks that are headed lower. Note: Look at a stock chart for a visual of the current trend. If a stock is below their 20-, 50-, or 100-day moving averages, and especially if it's below the almighty 200-day moving average, avoid buying.

Some people like to buy stocks on their way down, hoping to buy at the so-called bottom. Typically, stocks that are moving lower tend to keep going lower. It's very difficult to catch the bottom on any stock.

As I wrote earlier, save yourself time and money by sticking with underlying stocks that are steadily rising rather than falling. You can always consider buying a stock that has fallen but reverses direction. Once that stock has moved higher and proven itself, consider selling covered calls on it.

THE IDEAL MARKET ENVIRONMENT FOR SELLING CALLS

An excellent market environment for selling covered calls is similar to the kind of stocks you want to buy. In other words, it's slightly bullish and in a steady *uptrend* (i.e., the market is moving higher). A sideways market is also an acceptable environment for covered call sellers as long as the premium is not too low.

Conclusion

In this chapter, you learned that selling covered calls in a flat or slightly rising market is desirable for covered call sellers. Sure, there may be investors who disagree with this suggestion, and that's fine. As you gain more experience, you will choose your own criteria as which stocks are best for selling covered calls, and which market environment is satisfactory.

In Chapter 4, you'll learn the specific steps to take when selling a covered call. Once you see how it's done, I'm hoping you'll get as excited as I did the first time I discovered this brilliant strategy.

The next chapter is important because you learn the mechanics of this strategy. (As every teacher knows, the best way to learn how to do something is to actually do it.) Be sure to bring your "A" game before continuing!

CHAPTER 4

STEP-BY-STEP: SELLING A COVERED CALL

In this very important chapter, I show you the actual steps needed to sell a covered call. If this is the first time you've made a covered call trade, this chapter should be interesting. By the time you finish, you should know how to make a covered call trade.

As I take you through the steps below, the terminology you learned in previous chapters will make more sense. I'll even introduce a few more important words.

Reminder: Before you can sell a covered call, you must own at least 100 shares of stock whose options are available for trading. In our example, we already own 100 shares of Coca-Cola (KO). Because we own those 100 shares, we can sell 1 covered call on KO.

Let's discuss each of the steps needed to sell a covered call. I will start by displaying the November 29 option chain for Coca-Cola, which is one month away from our example date, October 29. Coca-Cola is selling for $65.78 per share.

Coca-Cola at $65.78 per share with a November 29th expiration date

65.78 -0.88 (-1.33%)

As of 1:42 PM EDT. Market Open.

Nov 29, 2024 ⌄ | All Strike Prices ⌄ | List ⌄ | Calls ⌄

Calls

Contract Name	Last Trade Date (EDT)	Strike	Last Price	Bid	Ask
KO241129C00060000	10/21/2024 5:44 PM	60	10.04	5.60	6.25
KO241129C00061000	10/29/2024 4:47 PM	61	5.10	4.90	5.30
KO241129C00062000	10/16/2024 1:38 PM	62	8.60	4.15	4.30
KO241129C00063000	10/24/2024 1:55 PM	63	5.10	3.30	3.40
KO241129C00064000	10/25/2024 7:49 PM	64	3.45	2.17	2.76
KO241129C00065000	10/29/2024 2:17 PM	65	1.85	1.75	1.81
KO241129C00066000	10/29/2024 2:34 PM	66	1.32	1.15	1.22
KO241129C00067000	10/29/2024 4:07 PM	67	0.70	0.68	0.73
KO241129C00068000	10/29/2024 5:03 PM	68	0.40	0.37	0.42
KO241129C00069000	10/29/2024 4:49 PM	69	0.19	0.19	0.22

Figure 4.1: Coca-Cola Option Chain
Source: Yahoo Finance

Before selling a covered call, you have many alternatives. You can pick any underlying stock, expiration date, strike price, or option premium that meets your needs. In the steps below, I'll take you through a typical covered call trade.

1. Start by signing onto your brokerage account. The first screen that appears is an account screen (it may also be called a "dashboard"). Somewhere on the

page you should see a "Trade" tab. After pressing "Trade," you should see an "Options" tab. Note: Every broker has different wording but they should all have a "Trade" tab and an "Options" tab.

2. Most importantly, you should see a box or line where you enter the underlying stock symbol. In our example, we will enter KO (for Coca-Cola).
3. After entering the stock symbol, KO, doublecheck to see that you are on the trading options screen. Important: You do not want to be on the stock trading screen when trading options!
4. After confirming that you entered the correct stock symbol, and that the options trading screen is displayed, select the *option chain* for KO (some brokers may refer to it as a *chain*.)
5. If done correctly, the call option chain for Coca Cola is displayed. It should look similar to Figure 4.1.
6. We chose the November 29 expiration date, which is exactly one month away. That gives us a decent amount of time before the call option expires. Many covered call sellers aim for an expiration date that is 30 to 45 days away, but it's a personal choice.

Note on expiration dates: Choosing a good expiration date is an important decision. On one hand, if you choose a date that is too far in the future (for example, three months), then your stock is "tied up" for a longer than necessary time period. As you may remember, after you sell a covered call on your stock, the call option buyer is in control of the stock until the expiration date. Because your stock is tied-up, you are not allowed to sell it until the option buyer frees you from the contract on or before the expiration date. (However, it is possible to close the contract and take back control of your stock, discussed in Chapter 6.)

On the other hand, if you choose a date that is too early such as one that arrives in one week, the premium may not be enough to meet your investing needs. Until you gain more experience, I'd suggest sticking with the 30- to 45-day time period for the expiration date.

7. Next, we have to choose a strike price. In Figure 4.1, strike prices for KO options range from a 60 to 100 (not shown on the screen). You already know that choosing the right strike price is important. Many covered call sellers adopt a strategy of selecting a strike price that is a few points above the current stock price. Others think in terms of percentages, which is something I recommend. When you measure your success in percentage terms (ROI), then it is best to evaluate profit potential in percentage terms.

8. In Figure 4.1, the bid price ranges from $5.60 for a 60 strike down to $.19 for the KO (Nov 29) 69 call. Keep in mind that the option prices constantly change, just as the underlying stock price does.

Since we're discussing premium, let me interrupt for a few minutes to discuss the amount of money collected when selling one covered call. As you'll see, the math is very basic.

Calculating premium

Remember that calculating the potential (i.e., maximum possible) profit is not the same as making money. One day after selling a covered call, the cash (premium) goes into your brokerage account (probably into a money market account). On the statement, it should be marked as "Credit Received" (although your broker may use different wording).

For some people, it's exciting to collect a premium for the very first time when selling an option. Here are the calculations, and it's straightforward.

Calculation #1:

If you sell one option contract (equal to 100 shares of stock) for $.68, you'll receive a $68 premium (100 shares x $.68).

Calculation #2:

If you sell one option contract for $1.15, you'll receive a $115 premium (100 shares x $1.15). When selling 3 call option contracts (equal to 300 shares), you receive $345 (300 shares x $1.15).

Note: For the sake of simplicity, in these examples we sell at the published bid price. In real life, however, you can negotiate for a higher price such as $1.20 or $1.19 in the above example. A lot depends on the bid-ask spread, or the highest published price someone is willing to pay for the option (i.e., bid price) and the lowest price at which someone is willing to sell that option (i.e., ask price). In fact, I do not recommend always selling at the bid price.

Now that you have a better idea of how much premium you may receive, let's continue with the steps.

9. After analyzing the option chain, we decide to write (sell) the November 29 call option with a 67 strike. The bid price is $.68 per share. Therefore, we receive a $68 premium for selling one covered call.

10. To place the trade, look for the words, SELL TO OPEN on the brokerage screen. The Sell to Open trade may also be as part of a dropdown menu below "Action." When you select Sell to Open, you are telling the computer to sell one (1) covered call on Coca-Cola (KO) with a strike price of 67, expiring at the close of business on November 29 of the current year at $.68.

    Note: In options terminology "Sell to Open" means opening or creating a new position when selling any option, including covered calls. This transaction means selling a call (or a put) that you do not own.

11. After you press the Enter key, there should be a review screen. Please check that all the information is correct, including the stock symbol. This is the best place to eliminate trade errors. Some investors accidentally try to sell covered calls on stocks they do not own, which is not only risky, but the trade will almost certainly be rejected by the computer.

12. After reviewing the transaction, press the "Confirm" or "Trade" button. After pressing the Enter key and after you receive a confirmation that the trade has been executed, in this example you will receive $68 the next business day. That cash is

deposited into your money market account at the brokerage firm.

13. Congratulations! There is not much more to do until the expiration date. One day after the trade, verify that you are "short" one KO 67 Nov 29 call option and the cash has been deposited into your account.

Buy-Write

On your trading screen, you may see a button or tab with the title, "Buy-Write." Pressing the Buy-Write button allows you to buy the underlying stock and write (sell) a covered call simultaneously. The Buy-Write button is there for your convenience, allowing investors to make a covered call trade in one transaction.

Note: You may be required to pay two commissions: one for buying stock, and another for selling the call. Although commissions are dramatically lower than they were in the past, options traders must still pay commissions for each trade. When calculating how the final profit or loss for the covered call (or any other) options trade, don't forget to include commissions.

GETTING PAID TO OWN A STOCK

The first time you receive premium, it's exciting. As one reader wrote, "I feel like I'm getting paid to own a stock." Actually, that's exactly what it feels like. However, like any strategy, there are risks as well as benefits. (The risks of selling covered calls will be discussed in Chapter 7.)

As you can see in the steps above, it's easy to sell a covered call. However, to achieve a desirable gain (and avoid potential problems), there are other things to know. Let's start by taking a closer look at choosing a good strike price. To do that, you must learn the meaning of *at-, in-, and out-of-the-money*.

At-, In-, and Out-of-the-Money

There are a number of nuances to selling covered calls, including understanding *in-the-money*, *out-of-the-money*, and *at-the-money* call options. These terms refer to the relationship between the strike price of the option and that of the underlying stock.

By the time you finish this chapter, you should be familiar with this terminology. Some readers may wonder why it's useful to learn these terms. Be patient, as this will make a lot more sense when we analyze covered call trades in Chapter 6.

At-the-money (ATM) options

Rule: When the current price of the stock is the *same* as the option strike price, the call option is said to be *at the money* (ATM). Even if the stock price is a few pennies away, its call option is still considered to be at the money.

Looking at the option chart in Figure 4.1, if KO is trading at $65 per share, and you select 65 as the strike price, the call option is *at the money*.

Note: The expiration date is irrelevant in this discussion.

Look at the chart below, which shows at-, in-, and out of the money. In this chart, the stock price is currently $40 per share.

At-, in-, and out-of-the-money chart

Stock Price	Strike Price	Call Option	Bid price
$40	$50	Far out of the money	$0.10
$40	$45	Out of the money	$0.40
$40	$42	Out of the money	$1.30
$40	$40	At the money	$2.70
$40	$35	In the money	$5.30
$40	$30	Deep in the money	$10.00

Figure 4.2: At-, in-, and out-of-the money

OUT OF THE MONEY

Rule: When the strike price of a call option is *higher* than the price of the underlying stock, the call option is *out of the money* (OTM).

In Figure 4.2, the stock price is $40 per share. The next strike price above $40 is out of the money. In this example, the 42 strike is two points away. The 45 strike is also out of the money (by 5 points). The expiration date doesn't matter because any strike above 40 is out of the money (in this example).

Hint: The higher the strike price, the further out of the money is the call option. The higher the strike price, the *lower* the premium. For example, the 42 call option has a bid price of $1.30 while the 45 strike is a paltry $.40. Therefore, the 42 strike is more valuable than the 45 strike (and investors are willing to pay a higher price for that option).

In the Money

Rule: When the strike price of a call option is *lower* than the price of the underlying stock, the call option is *in the money* (ITM).

As you can see in Figure 4.2, the next closest call option with a strike price *below* $40 per share is the 35 strike. That option is in the money by 5 points. Any strike price below 40 is in the money. The deeper the call option is in the money, the higher the premium.

Note: Just because an option is in the money doesn't necessarily mean that the option buyer will earn a profit. The only factor that determines whether there is a profit is whether the sale price is higher than the purchase price. The term, "in the money," simply refers to the relationship between the strike price and the stock price. It does *not* refer to whether anyone made a profit.

You just learned about knowing whether a call option is in-, out of-, or at the money. Only in-the-money options are exercised by their owner when expiration arrives. When that happens, the option writer sells their stock at the strike price. If the option is out of the money, then you get to keep the stock.

Which Call Option to Sell?

That's the million-dollar question!

In fact, there are two main strategies that option writers use. For beginners, I suggest starting with the bullish strategy of selling out-of-the-money calls. This concept is the easiest for covered call writers to understand because it allows for the possibility of earning money directly from an increase in the price of the stock.

The strike price of the chosen option makes a difference in how much premium you'll receive (although volatility and time to expiration are just as important).

Fortunately, I'll show you how to sell in-the-money calls in Chapter 6 when I go over a number of actual trade examples. To be clear, selling out-of-the-money calls should be the first covered call strategy to learn. After getting your feet wet with out-of-the-money calls, some readers may want to sell at-the-money calls. Most important, after gaining a better understanding of how selling covered calls works, choose an option with any strike price that meets your needs.

Bottom line: In the example above, the out-of-the-money call with a strike of 42 can be sold for $1.30 (bid price), an appropriate choice for most investors.

Advanced note: If you choose the 42 strike, it means you are obligated to sell the stock at $42 per share if the call buyer "exercises" their right. We'll discuss this in Chapter 5.

KEEP A JOURNAL

If you trade stocks or options, I encourage you to keep a journal of your trades. When selling covered calls, include important information such as the underlying stock, the strike price, expiration date, premium received, maximum possible profit, and the reasons for choosing this trade.

When expiration passes, tabulate the total profit or loss. Finally, if you learned any lessons from the trade, include those in your journal as well, including details that may help with the next trade. The following is a sample journal entry.

Sample journal entry

500 shares of YYYY purchased at $24.50 on October 25.

Current stock price: $27.75 on December 21.

Strike price: 29

Expiration date: January 22.

Sold 5 calls at $1.61 each

Premium received: $805 (less commission).

Stock profit at expiration: $1,625 ($27.75 - $24.50 = 3.25 points x 500 shares)

Total profit at expiration: $2,430 ($1,625 + $805)

Details: The option expired worthless so the covered call seller gets to keep the stock.

CONCLUSION

This concludes the chapter on the steps involved when selling covered calls. As I said earlier, the mechanics of selling a covered call are relatively simple. The hard part is choosing an appropriate underlying stock, the option's strike price, and expiration date.

In Chapter 5, you will learn about *assignment*, which occurs when the option is in the money at expiration. In reality, assignment is a simple process. Briefly, when the option was sold, you gave someone the right to buy your stock, and they decided to do so. Assignment is simply a notice informing you that the option owner exercised their option.

To make sure there is no confusion, in the next chapter, I explain assignment in more detail.

CHAPTER 5

ASSIGNMENT: THE OBLIGATION TO SELL YOUR SHARES

At a certain date and time listed in the contract, expiration day arrives and the option expires. Once the expiration date arrives, one of two good things happen for the covered call seller: First, the call option may expire worthless (it is OTM) and you continue to hold the stock. Or, second, the stock is *called away* (i.e., sold at the strike price), locking in your maximum profit for the trade. Either outcome is positive.

Officially, when a stock is "called away," it means that you were "assigned," and are obligated to sell the stock at the strike price. Don't worry because this all happens automatically behind the scenes.

You don't have to do anything except to know that when selling covered calls, there is a chance it will be called away, i.e., sold at the strike price that you chose. (Note: I will be repeating these terms several times in this chapter.)

WHEN DO OPTIONS EXPIRE?

When exactly do options expire? The expiration date is included in the contract, but the option typically ceases to exist on the third Friday of each month at 4 p.m. ET, when the market closes.

Other options, such as *weekly options*, expire on other dates. The expiration date can be seen in the option chain. Note: Weekly options are discussed at the end of this chapter.

AS THE EXPIRATION DATE APPROACHES

As mentioned several times, if the option owner elects to buy your shares that they "rented" from you on the expiration date (or earlier), you keep the premium and the proceeds from the stock sale. You can always repurchase the stock and sell another covered call. A lot of experienced covered call sellers do this: They wait until the stock is sold on the expiration date, then they buy the stock again and sell new covered calls. (This is a choice, not a recommendation.)

If the option buyer does *not* exercise their right to buy the stock (because the option is out of the money on the expiration date), then you keep the premium and the stock. Once again, you can sell another covered call when the market next opens for trading.

As expiration approaches, it's important to have an *exit plan*. You don't want to wait until the last minute to discover that your stock was unexpectedly called away. However, if your plan was for the stock to be sold, then your strategy was successful.

Another word for a stock that is called away is *assignment*. The option seller is said to have been "assigned an exercise notice."

Understanding Assignment

To clarify, if a stock is called away or you are *assigned*, it means the stock is taken out of your account and is replaced with the cash generated from the stock sale. That amount is 100 x the option strike price. As mentioned earlier, an option that is out of the money on the expiration date will almost never be exercised.

Let's discuss in more detail what happens when you are assigned an exercise notice.

Your Obligation as a Covered Call Seller

As a covered call seller, you have an important obligation. If the option owner chooses to exercise their rights (typically when the call option is in the money at expiration), you are obligated to sell your underlying stock at the strike price. You, as the option seller, will be *assigned* an exercise notice. ((By the way, the assignment notice comes from the OCC (Options Clearing Corporation). They are just letting you know that your stock has already been sold.))

Note: Founded in 1973, the OCC is the agency that regulates, clears, and settles listed option trades for the U.S. stock options market. They operate under the jurisdiction of the SEC (Securities and Exchange Commission.)

If the random option buyer decides to *exercise* the call option (which is the right that you sold to them), they are allowed to buy your stock at the strike price. This is according to the option contract.

As a covered call seller, it is theoretically possible to have your stock called away at any time, but it's almost always done at expiration. Don't expect assignment before expiration, although it may happen, such as prior to the ex-dividend date when the dividend is high enough to make that choice attractive.

Here's the good news: As a covered call seller, assignment is a good outcome. It means your strategy worked. If you are going to sell covered calls, be prepared to have your stock called away. This is another reason why choosing a suitable strike price is so important.

However, if you can't stand the idea of having your stock sold on the expiration date, then find another strategy. Many people sell covered calls on stocks they planned to sell. Their stock is sold, plus they also received income (premium). This is why this strategy is so popular.

Note: If your stock is called away, it is done automatically. There is nothing for you to do. You will be notified by your broker that you were assigned an exercise notice and no longer own the stock. Again, you can always repurchase the stock, and sell covered calls for the next month.

WHAT HAPPENS IF YOUR STOCK IS NOT CALLED AWAY?

1. You can continue to hold the stock and sell covered calls on the same stock with a later expiration.
2. You can sell the stock outright (because your obligation expired with the call).
3. Prior to expiration, you can ROLL over the option by closing the option position and opening (i.e., selling)

another call. Rolling an option will be discussed in Chapter 6.

Have an Exit Plan

Many people believe that after selling a covered call, all they have to do is wait until expiration. While waiting, it is wise to periodically monitor the underlying stock to be certain that it still belongs in your portfolio.

Once the option expires, you'll learn the option owner's decision. As you remember, the option buyer has two choices: to let the option expire, or to buy the underlying stock at the strike. If they do buy the underlying stock, you'll be assigned an exercise notice (see below).

Review: Exercise and Assignment

For those who need a brief summary of what was discussed above, the following should meet your needs. It also includes a few more details.

1. For assignment to occur, the call buyer (also called the call holder) must exercise the option. Put another way, the buyer submits an exercise notice to their broker. Then the broker notifies the OCC, which assigns the notice to a random person who sold that option.
2. Once the buyer submits an exercise notice, assignment notices are distributed, and the stock is sold at the strike price.
3. There is nothing to do. The stock is delivered from

your account to that of the exerciser. It's all done automatically by the OCC and your broker.

4. In the real world, you could wake up Monday morning after expiration and unexpectedly discover that the stock is no longer in your account because it was called away at the strike price. This happens when the owner decided to exercise their right to buy the stock.

5. In summary, exercise and assignment are paired. You can't have one without the other.

6. Once again, assignment is welcomed by covered call sellers because the strategy worked just as designed. Unfortunately, some beginners who don't understand the process are surprised when their stock is sold.

Note to European readers: European-style options can only be exercised *on* the expiration date, and not before. American-style options, although almost always exercised on the expiration date, can be exercised before the expiration date. In this book, we only discuss trading American-style options.

THE UNEXERCISED OPTION

What happens when the strike price is above the stock price (i.e., the call option is out of the money)? In this case, the option expires and becomes worthless on the expiration date. By the way, this happens far more often than many people think. Nevertheless, if the option does not get exercised by the buyer, you get to keep the stock and "pocket the premium." This is when the profit is officially locked in.

For many covered call sellers, this is a great outcome. After all, you already received the premium for the call option. Now you keep the stock and can sell other calls. In fact, some covered call sellers secretly hope the stock never makes it to the strike price on the expiration date and the option expires worthless.

Early Assignment

There are exceptions to when a stock is called away. On rare occasions, a stock will be called away *before* the expiration date. For example, a trader may want to capture an impending dividend on the underlying stock and exercise the call option at the close of business on the day before the stock goes ex-dividend.

When this happens, your stock will be called away and you will not get the dividend. Therefore, it's wise to be aware of the possibility for early assignment but in reality, it rarely happens.

Once in a while, call buyers make a mistake and exercise the option as soon as the stock price is above the strike price, even by pennies. This is a huge mistake, so do not expect it to happen, although it's possible.

Preparing for Assignment

When selling covered calls, you expect and plan for assignment. When your stock is called away, your strategy was a success. You knew your stock could be taken out of your account and sold at the strike price.

If for some reason, you don't want your stock called away (perhaps for tax reasons or you think the stock will explode higher), you probably shouldn't be selling covered calls in the first place. Nevertheless, you can avoid assignment by buying back the option.

Introducing Weekly options

Although this book is primarily aimed at selling covered calls that expire each month, this is a good time to mention that you can sell covered calls on weekly options (also referred to as "Weeklys").

Weekly options typically expire on a Monday, Wednesday, or Friday (depending on the product). Weekly's come with increased risks because the expiration dates are so short. In addition, the premium from weekly options is smaller.

However, many people who sell weekly covered calls love the fact that they receive income (i.e., cash flow) at a faster rate and with a higher annual ROI (return on investment). Instead of once a month, income is theoretically coming into their account every week or two.

There are a number of disadvantages to selling the Weeklys. First, not all underlying stocks or ETFs have weekly options (only the most actively traded ones do). Second, it takes a lot more work to manage risk because the option prices are smaller (due to their short lifetime), and more volatile (again, because of their short lifetime).

Which is more profitable, selling a monthly covered call or a Weekly? With a standard monthly option, you'll receive higher income upfront. With a Weekly, although the premium is usually lower, you can expect to receive more premium over time (higher ROI), even though it takes more effort.

Bottom line: There is no best option to sell. If you're a beginner, it's wise to avoid short-term options until you have gained a lot more experience and confidence. That means knowing when an option position has become too risky to hold.

After that, you can always try to trade the Weeklys and see if it fits your trading schedule, temperament, and risk tolerance. For most people, selling monthly covered calls provides the right balance. The premium is higher and it's a lot less work to initiate and monitor.

CONCLUSION

I hope that you have a better grasp of the two-step process of exercise and assignment. For the covered call seller, assignment is the only action that affects them.

In Chapter 6, we will take all of the knowledge learned so far and apply it to several real-life trades. The trade examples include stocks that may move in the right direction (higher), the wrong direction (lower), or remain near the same price level. I think you'll find this chapter extremely useful. It should also clear up any confusion you have about how this strategy works in real life.

Chapter 6

Trades That Go Right, Wrong, or Sideways

By now, you should have a good idea of how to sell covered calls for weekly or monthly income. Nevertheless, there is much more to learn. In this important chapter, I walk you through several covered call trades while analyzing what could go right, wrong, or sideways.

Although selling covered calls is a relatively straightforward way to make money, there are unexpected events that may create complications. I want you to be prepared for these events, especially if the underlying stock price moves in an unexpected direction.

In many trading books, you'll read about perfect entry and exit scenarios that give you the highest possible pretend profits. The problem, however, is that what happens in a book often does not carry over into a real-life trade.

Fortunately, there aren't too many things that can go wrong when selling covered calls, one of the reasons I recommend this strategy. It's less complicated, and it's easy to get out of bad trades. Typically, the biggest risk takes place when the stock price plunges unexpectedly.

Nevertheless, there are times when a covered call trade goes so far off track that it needs your immediate attention. Beginning now, I go over a number of good, bad, and sideways scenarios. Studying the following examples may help you appreciate the thinking that is needed before making a trade.

Example #1 (ITM):
The stock price moves slightly above the strike price at expiration

We purchased the underlying stock, Coca-Cola (KO) when it was selling for $65.81 per share, and sold 1 call with a strike of 67. KO is now trading for $68.45 per share one day before expiration. Coca Cola's call options are in the money by 1.45 points.

Reminder: Even if the underlying stock is above the strike price by as little as $.01 (the call option is in the money), the stock will almost certainly be called away at expiration.

In this bullish example, if KO remains above $67 per share on expiration day, you will be assigned an exercise notice and the stock will be sold at $67 per share. You keep the premium received a month ago plus all of the proceeds from selling the stock.

Analysis: This is a positive scenario. If KO's call options are in the money on the expiration date, the stock is sold at the strike price. This locks in the maximum possible gain for this trade. You can always buy KO again, or invest the proceeds in any other stock, and sell another call with a new strike price and expiration date. Congratulations on a successful trade.

On occasion, some investors second guess their trades. In this example, although they were willing to sell the stock at

$67, after it happens, it annoys them that they missed out on any stock gains above $67.

Hopefully, after reading this book, you won't fall into that trap. Accept that the stock was sold at the strike price and don't think about how much money you "could have, should have, or would have" made if you had not sold a covered call.

Example #1 Calculations (ITM)

The following is an example of a journal entry for Example #1.

Bought 100 shares of KO purchased at $65.81 on February 14, 2025.
Current stock price: $68.45 date
Strike price: 67
Expiration date: March 25, 2025
Sold 1 KO call contract at $.68
Premium received: $68
Stock profit: +$119 (67 strike - $65.81 purchase price = 1.19 points)
Total profit: +$187 ($119 + $68)

EXAMPLE #2 (ITM): THE STOCK MOVES WILDLY HIGHER ABOVE THE STRIKE PRICE AT EXPIRATION (THE CALL OPTION IS IN THE MONEY)

We purchased the underlying stock, Coca-Cola (KO) when it was selling for $65.81 per share, and sold 1 call with a strike of 67. KO is now trading at $71.75 per share one day before expiration. In this profitable but not ideal scenario, Coca Cola's call options are in the money by 4.75 points.

Since KO is well above the strike price a day before expiration, the buyer will exercise the option tomorrow (expiration day), and pay $67 for your stock.

Analysis: Although you received premium for selling the call option, and received the proceeds from selling the stock at $67 per share (the strike price), you won't receive any profits on the stock price above $67 no matter how high KO goes. Any profit past the strike price is not yours, which is one of the downsides of selling covered calls.

As you know, you're not aiming to hit a home run when selling covered calls, Instead, the goal is to collect a decent premium again and again and compound those earnings.

Example #2 Calculations (ITM)

The following is an example of a more detailed journal entry for Example #2.

Trade Date to Open: 10/25/2024
Buy 100 KO @ $65.81; Cost $6,581
Sell 1 KO (Nov 29) 67 call @ 0.68; Net Cash: $68
Position Cost (Stock Price minus Option Premium): $6,513

Trade Date to Close: 11/29/2024 (expiration)
Sell 100 KO @ $67.00 via assignment
Net Proceeds when closing: $6,700
Profit: (Proceeds minus Cost) $187
ROI (Profit/Cost) = 2.79%

Bottom line: As you can see by the calculations above, this was a profitable trade.

Now, let's look at a simple calculation that will help determine whether your covered call strategy is working.

Calculating breakeven

This simple calculation, usually done before you initiate the trade, shows the profit range for the position. In other words, as long as the underlying stock is above the calculated breakeven price, the covered call trade will show a profit.

Whether the option is in- at- or out-of-the-money, the breakeven price is the price paid for the underlying stock minus the option premium.

Example

$65.78 Stock price
– .68 premium
$65.10 breakeven price

In Example #1 and #2, because the stock price was above the breakeven price on the expiration date, the trades were profitable.

Now that you know how to calculate breakeven, let's see what happens when the underlying stock falls slightly below the strike price near the expiration date.

EXAMPLE #3 OTM:

THE UNDERLYING STOCK FINISHES SLIGHTLY BELOW THE STRIKE PRICE. THE CALL OPTION IS OUT OF THE MONEY AT EXPIRATION

When the underlying stock finishes below the call's strike price at expiration, you keep the stock. For many covered call writers, this is an ideal scenario. They can sell another call option for the following month.

Example #3 Calculations (OTM)

The following is an example of a basic journal entry for Example #3.

100 shares KO purchased at $65.81
Current stock price: $66.25
Strike price: 67
Expiration date: November 29
Sold 1 call contract at $.68
Premium received: $68
Stock gain: $44 ($66.25 stock price - $65.81 purchase price = .44 points)
Total gain: $112 ($44 + $68)

Bottom line: This was another profitable trade.

Example #4: The Underlying Stock Is Plunging Before the Expiration Date (OTM)

A worst-case scenario for covered call sellers is when they're holding a stock that sinks at any time prior to expiration. In this case, the premium received provides partial financial relief, but it's not enough to offset the entire loss.

That's when some investors may feel trapped in a losing position and believe they can't get out. Fortunately, there is a way to close a covered call position and free the stock for sale (explained later in this chapter). Dumping the stock may be done when the stockholder feels they must sell the shares. Usually, panic makes for a poor trade decision, but this is a personal choice.

Note: Some people correctly state that a falling stock price is one risk for covered call sellers. Guess what? That's the same risk shared by all stockholders. However, covered call sellers lose less because their losses are reduced by the premium received.

Example #4 Calculations (OTM)

The following is an example of a basic journal entry for Example #4.

100 shares KO purchased at $65.81
Current stock price: $61
Strike price: 67
Expiration date: November 29
Sold 1 call contract at $.68
Premium received: $68
Position cost: $6,513
Position loss: $6,100 - $6,513 = -$413

Analysis: The major risk of selling covered calls is that the underlying stock price drops by a huge sum. For example, when KO declined to $61 (from $65.81), it was far below both the 67 strike and the initial position cost. The call option is far out of the money and the option expires worthless.

Although the stockholder lost money on this position, the premium provided a little downside protection. It's not fun to lose that much money, so it's worth examining why the stock fell by so much and whether you still want to own these shares.

If your stock price is moving lower, and you believe there is little chance of recovery, there are some steps you can take. Here are some ideas.

When the Underlying Stock Price Is Plunging

It's not a pleasant experience when your underlying stock falls below the trade breakeven price and enters the abyss. Some covered call sellers panic when this happens, which almost always results in an unforced error.

Here are some actions you can take if your underlying stock is plunging:

1. You can do nothing. You already received a premium for writing the call. At expiration, you will still be holding the stock, but at a much lower price. You can sell another call on the same stock for the next month, and once again, receive premium for doing so. However, it may be painful (but necessary) to choose a strike price below your original breakeven price.

2. While doing nothing, you can "hope" that your plunging stock rebounds before the expiration date, and returns at or near the strike price. As you probably know, "hoping" is never a good strategy. However, being patient makes sense when you decide that the stock is worth holding despite its price behavior. Perhaps the pullback is only temporary.

3. You can buy additional shares as the price falls. If this is a stock you want to own for the long term, perhaps you may welcome a pullback in the price. Then you can buy more shares at a lower price.

Note: "Buying the dip" is a relatively risky strategy because stocks that fall tend to keep falling. Nevertheless, if you want to buy the dip, feel free to do so, but only when you are confident the stock will recover. Unfortunately, few investors are good at predicting future stock direction.

4. You can close your call position and sell the underlying stock. The steps needed to do this are described in the sidebar below. You'd take this action because you don't expect the stock to recover anytime soon. This allows you to cut your losses.

Buy Back: How to close a covered call position before expiration

You always have the option (pun intended) to buy back any option that you sold earlier to close the position. The reason for taking this step is to regain control of your stock before the expiration date. Then you can unload the shares or sell a new option with a lower strike price and collect a higher premium. This is not a frequently-used strategy but you should know how it works.

Keep in mind that buying back a call option on a losing stock means giving back some of the premium. That is in addition to incurring a loss when selling the stock. After buying back the call option, you take control of the stock.

Here are the simple steps to buy back a call option:

1. Enter the option symbol on your brokerage options order entry screen.
2. Select Buy to Close (purchase an option to close a short position).

3. Enter the current ask price (or try to buy at a lower price).
4. After pressing the Enter key, and after receiving a trade confirmation, you are free from the terms of the option contract. You can continue to own the stock or sell it.

Note: Some covered call sellers buy back the option on a rallying stock because they want to prevent the stock from being called away. Yes, they lose money on the trade, but perhaps they want to hold the stock longer, or they want to avoid a capital gains tax issue, but for whatever reason, they don't want to be assigned.

Bottom line:
What is the best-case scenario for covered call sellers?

The consensus from many covered call sellers is to have the option finish slightly out of the money, which allows them to continue holding the stock. Then they can sell a new covered call for the following month.

If slightly bullish, then by all means sell out-of-the-money calls. However, if you have no opinion about the stock's direction, and want more protection in case the stock falls, then consider selling ATM or ITM calls.

Remember that no matter which strategy you use, when selling covered calls, you must be willing to sell your stock at the strike price.

TRADING SUGGESTION: START SMALL WITH ONLY 1 CONTRACT

One of the best ways to learn how to sell covered calls is by selling only 1 call contract at a time. As you gain experience using this strategy, and you want to sell more than 1 contract, feel free to do so, as long as you own at least 100 shares for each call sold.

USE THE OPTIONS MARKET TO SELL STOCK THAT YOU OWN

One clever way to sell your stocks is to use the options market. For example, let's say you own 100 shares of YYYY, which is now selling for $71 per share. You have been wanting to sell this stock for a long time with a target price of $73.

Example #1: Instead of selling the stock for $71, you check the bid price for the 73 strike, which is $1.40, and choose a 45-day expiration date. In this example, you receive $140 in premium. If the stock is called away and sold at $73 per share, your plan worked. You sold the stock at your target price and made a few extra dollars.

A problem occurs when the stock rises above $73, only to decline again before expiration. That leaves you stuck with the stock. As covered call writers, that is the risk we are willing to take. See the next example for a trade idea that increases your chance to get that stock for $73 per share.

Example #2: A wiser move is to sell the $70 call for at least $3.00, netting $73 for your stock, assuming assignment. This time the stock price must be only above $70 on the expiration date.

This strategy works best when you want to sell the stock but are not in a hurry to do so. As long as there isn't a severe market decline over the next month or two, the strategy is a clever way of eliminating stock positions from your portfolio, and receiving a price that is above the current market price.

"Rollin,' rollin,' rollin'..."

In the old TV series, *Rawhide*, starring Clint Eastwood, rollin' referred to cowboys keeping the cattle constantly moving on a cattle drive. In the options world, "rolling" refers to closing one option position and opening another.

Rolling an option

When rolling an option position, close the call you are currently short and open a new option position with a different strike price and later expiration date. There are a number of rolling strategies available.

Roll up

If you don't want your stock to be called away on the expiration date, you can *roll up* to an option with a higher strike price. Your new option position may have any expiration date, but the strike price has changed.

For example, let's say you sold 5 YYYY March 69 calls. When YYYY hits $68.50 per share, you don't want your stock to be called away (hopefully, for a good reason). Next, buy back the March calls at, or near, the current ask price and close the option position (select Buy to Close on your brokerage screen). You can now sell 5 calls at a higher strike price such as March 71 or April 71. This gives your stock more room to move higher, and with less chance of being called away.

ROLL OUT OR ROLL FORWARD

A roll out (or roll forward) allows you to sell more calls on the same stock. For example, let's say you are still holding a short position with 5 YYYY March 69 calls. In this example, you may decide that the March 69 calls are so inexpensive that they offer essentially zero downside protection. Your plan is to establish a new covered call position with a more substantial premium. Therefore, you "roll out" the 5 March options to April 69 (or a different strike price). Close the March 69s and simultaneously sell to open the April 69s.

CONCLUSION

After studying these sample trades, I am confident you have a better idea of how to sell covered calls. Obviously, when making real trades, anything is possible. For many readers, it's prudent to gain experience by making a number of covered call trades. Once again, I encourage you to begin with only one contract for each stock.

In the next chapter, we will go over the risks and disadvantages of selling covered calls. Fortunately, there aren't that many, but it's important to know what they are.

CHAPTER 7

DISADVANTAGES AND RISKS

After reading this far, you may think that selling covered calls is too good to be true. There must be a catch somewhere, right? As I wrote previously, selling covered calls is one of the less risky options strategies, but it doesn't mean there is no risk. In reality, there are a few manageable risks, and some disadvantages, when selling covered calls.

Below, I discuss a few of these disadvantages and risks with suggested solutions. Many of these shortcomings have been discussed briefly in previous chapters, but it's worth taking a closer look.

WHAT IS RISK?

Before discussing the potential risks of using this strategy, I'd like to define it. Here is what risk is: It's the sum that can be lost on any trade. Whenever you are involved in any financial market, be aware that it's possible to lose money. This is the risk that all investors and traders take.

If you don't want to take any risks at all, you may put your money in a fixed income investment such as a certificate of deposit (CD) or a money market account.

When investing in fixed income, it is almost certain that your principal (the original sum invested) is safe.

However, the return on your investment will be far less. You cannot expect a good return without some risk.

Now, let's begin our discussion.

RISK:
YOUR STOCK PLUNGES

If the underlying stock price declines substantially, then you'll lose money. It's not the fault of the option that you lost money. In fact, by selling a covered call and receiving a premium, your losses were reduced.

If you must assign blame, blame it on your choice for an underlying stock. Even without selling a covered call, you'd still lose money because the premium was not enough to cover the entire loss on the stock. By selling covered calls, however, you received some cash in return for renting that stock until expiration.

RISK:
YOU MISS OUT ON A RISING STOCK

As mentioned in previous chapters, one disadvantage of selling covered calls is you do not get to participate in the profits when the underlying stock rises well above the strike price. With this scenario, the stock will be called away on the expiration date and you will collect only the strike price.

In other words, although your stock might make a phenomenal move higher, all you can collect is the profit up to the strike price as you sit and watch your imaginary profits go to someone else.

Bottom line: One of the criticisms of selling covered calls is that gains are limited or capped at the strike price. In return for accepting that limitation, you receive premium. If you understand and accept this limitation, then you should do well in your covered call writing career. If this idea feels uncomfortable, perhaps this is not the right strategy for you at this time.

Reminder: If you're in the options market because you want to make a big, quick profit, then selling covered calls may not meet your needs. There are other option strategies that purport to achieve that goal (strategies that are explained in my bestselling book, *Understanding Options*).

DISADVANTAGE:
YOUR STOCK IS TIED UP (OR LOCKED UP) UNTIL THE EXPIRATION DATE

One of the limitations of this strategy is that the underlying stock can't be sold unless you *buy to close* the option position—or it expires. When selling a covered call, you sold the "right to buy the stock" to the option owner. All you can do is wait until you take back control of the stock.

As you learned in Chapter 6, although you have the right to buy back the option, it may require paying more for the option than you received when selling. Therefore, it's usually better to hold the stock until the expiration date (unless there is a strong reason to close the covered call position early and sell your stock).

DISADVANTAGE:
YOU NEED ENOUGH MONEY TO BUY 100 SHARES OF STOCK

While reading this book, many of you may get excited about the idea of renting out a stock and receiving income. However, to do so, you need enough money in your account to buy at least 100 shares of stock. For some, this may not be easy to do, at least at first. Not everyone has enough money in their account to buy 100 shares of a stock that is selling for at least $10 per share (you'll need at least $1,000 to buy one of these stocks).

If you don't have that much readily available cash for investment, that is not a huge problem. To get started with smaller sums, consider investing a few dollars every month into an index fund, such as the S&P 500 index mutual fund or ETF (exchange-traded fund). Eventually, when you have built enough capital, you can buy stocks, and then write covered calls.

Note: If you want to learn how to get started building wealth for yourself, children, or relatives, I recommend a book I wrote, *Help Your Child Build Wealth* (Wiley, 2024).

RISK:
IT FEELS LIKE A "CAN'T LOSE" STRATEGY

One of the risks with selling covered calls is that some investors think they will never lose money. Although it is an excellent, profit-making strategy, writing covered calls is not the Holy Grail.

Therefore, unless you are an excellent stock-picker, or you have never seen a bear market, believe me when I tell you that not all of your stocks are going to move sideways or higher. Some will decline. That is the risk we all take when we enter the financial markets.

Bottom line: This strategy is not for impatient investors who want a big, immediate return. In fact, other option strategies have reputations as being "get-rich-quick" schemes. Selling covered calls is not that strategy. It is for those who want to build long-term wealth by renting their stocks to the speculators who are looking to make fast money. With the covered call strategy, investors are happy to make profits but are not in a rush to make a fortune. They are willing to build income slowly.

Disadvantage: Selling covered calls is boring

For some people, selling covered calls is boring. They receive premium and then wait until the expiration date. That's when they find out if the stock was either called away or whether the option became worthless and expired.

Although patient, risk-adverse investors will appreciate selling covered calls because it brings in income, speculators looking for money and excitement will not like the strategy. It really depends on their personality and risk tolerance.

Risk: Accidentally selling "naked" calls

As you already know, when selling covered calls, you must own the stock. That is the definition of "covered." As mentioned earlier, when selling calls on stocks that you don't own, it's called "selling naked."

Selling naked calls is risky because potential losses are unlimited. For every point that the stock price moves above the strike price, the naked call seller loses $100. Simply put, if you sell a naked call option with a strike price equal to $60, and the stock zooms to $80, your loss would be $2,000 for each option sold. Because stocks do not have a theoretical upper limit, and because the loss can be much more than $2,000, brokerage firms do not allow most of their option clients to sell naked call options.

It's extremely difficult for someone to mistakenly sell naked calls, but here's how it could happen:

1. You log onto your brokerage screen and type in the symbol for your underlying stock.
2. However, instead of typing "KO" for Coca-Cola, you accidentally type "KR," the stock symbol for The Kroger Company.
3. If you sold 3 calls on Kroger at $1.25 each, you'd be selling 3 naked calls because you don't own 300 shares of KR stock. You'd receive $375 in premium.
4. Fortunately, your broker will almost certainly decline the transaction because selling naked calls is a sophisticated *bearish* strategy for experienced, and well-financed, traders. If the trade did go through, you'd be holding a very risky position. You'd also have to deposit a bunch of cash as a margin requirement for holding the position.

Bottom line: Be very careful when entering stock symbols on the brokerage screen. If you enter the wrong stock symbol, there may be negative consequences.

Why People Lose Money Selling Covered Calls

There are a number of reasons why some people lose money selling covered calls. Truthfully, this section can apply to nearly any financial transaction, including buying and selling stocks.

The following are the most common mistakes that investors make when selling covered calls.

1. **Investors get too emotional**

   When selling covered calls, there is a strong likelihood that the stock you own will be taken out of your account and sold at the strike price. If you fall in love with your stocks and hate the idea of selling, or you're worried about potential tax consequences from the sale, then you may want to find another strategy.

2. **Not paying attention to upcoming earnings announcements**

   If there is anything that can disrupt a covered call trade, it's an earnings announcement. That is why you should be aware of any "special events" such as earnings before the expiration date. Because these events can play havoc with a stock price, it's best to pay attention to any earnings news that may affect your stock. Then you can decide to make the trade, or not.

3. **Greed**

   Greed causes some rational, conservative covered call sellers to abandon the relatively tame covered call strategy for more speculative strategies.

Warning: As tempting as it may be to switch to higher-risk option strategies, unless you're willing to spend years studying options, stick to the easier-to-learn covered call strategy. Selling covered calls is for people who want to receive steady monthly checks from a "renter." The risks are less than with traditional stock ownership, but sometimes so are the gains. It's far less stressful to sell covered calls than to try to make a huge sum of money guessing which direction a stock may go.

4. Panic

Many traders, including covered call sellers, panic when the underlying stock, or the entire market, plunges. Fear causes them to hastily cover their short call and dump their stock at the wrong time.

When selling covered calls, or using any investment strategy, keep a level head and be unemotional about your trades. There's almost never a reason to make impulsive decisions, which often leads to lost money. Instead, evaluate your position and make decisions based on the facts, not emotions. The antidote for panic trading is creating a trading plan.

If you believe that your stock really has little chance of recovering, buy back the option and sell the stock. But this should be part of a well-thought-out plan, not a "rash decision." And never forget, if you decide a stock is no longer worth owning, you can always move to another stock.

MISCONCEPTIONS ABOUT OPTIONS

The following list of misconceptions may seem like a review to some readers, but remember that many people avoid options because of misinformation or emotions. This is a summary of those feelings and fallacies.

1. **"Options are too risky!"**

   Yes, some option strategies are high risk, but selling covered calls is not one of them. As mentioned several times, it is one of the less risky option strategies.

2. **"Options are too confusing!"**

   Similar to learning a new language, the options vocabulary can be confusing. Hopefully, after reading this book, the strategy makes more sense. If not, then re-read the vocabulary definitions in the first two chapters.

A great source for anything related to options trading is the Options Industry Council (OIC), the educational arm of the U.S. option exchanges and the Options Clearing Corporation (OCC). If you have questions about selling covered calls or any other option strategy, email them at options@theocc.com.

The staff is extremely knowledgeable and helpful, and they will answer every conceivable question (but don't ask for investment advice). Write or call if you get stuck on an idea while reading this book, or need help if in the middle of a covered call trade.

The OIC website, www.optionseducation.org, is filled with useful educational information including free online option classes, videos, webcasts, podcasts, research papers, and live seminars.

The CBOE (Chicago Board Options Exchange), is another excellent options educational source. They offer free online option courses, live seminars, podcasts, and webcasts.

Note: An excellent website for stock and option definitions is Investopedia (www.investopedia.com). A full list of educational websites can be found in the glossary.

3. "Isn't all option trading gambling?"

No. Selling covered calls is a responsible way to increase cash flow on stocks that you already own. Option strategies that are similar to gambling get a lot of media attention, one reason many people mistakenly think that all options strategies are speculative. In reality, many option strategies are designed to reduce risk (i.e., hedging).

4. "I was told to buy calls, not sell them."

Buying calls is a speculative strategy that is deceptively easy to learn. However, making consistent money with this strategy is extremely difficult. When buying calls (or puts), you must guess that the stock will move in the right direction in a short time, and know whether the options are reasonably priced. Most traders are unsuccessful at timing the market, one of the reasons that selling covered calls is such a popular strategy.

Conclusion

In the next chapter, I interview an options expert who gives fascinating insights into the covered call strategies that he uses. That includes the risks and benefits of writing covered calls, and sound advice on how to increase income while limiting losses.

This is a must-read chapter. Even if you think you know almost everything about selling covered calls, there is a lot to learn from an experienced options trader who began writing covered calls in the 1970's.

CHAPTER 8

BEYOND THE BASICS: INTERVIEW WITH AN EXPERT

I was fortunate that a retired options expert with over 30 years' experience on the CBOE (Chicago Board Options Exchange) agreed to discuss all aspects of the covered call strategy with me. He agreed to the interview provided that I don't reveal his name.

I believe you can gain a lot of useful knowledge about selling covered calls from reading this interview. With my questions, I made sure that this covered call writer was able to clarify and reinforce much of the information included in this book. Even better, he not only reinforced many of the concepts but went beyond the basics.

In the interview, he discussed his favorite covered call method, the mistakes many covered call writers make, ways to reduce risk, why assignment should not be feared, and a brief conversation about *intrinsic value*, *time value*, *historical volatility*, *implied volatility*, and the *Greeks*. At the end of the chapter, I explain these concepts in more detail.

I am certain you will find this interview useful whether you are a beginner or experienced covered call writer. Keep in mind that some of the ideas he discusses are aimed at intermediate option traders.

Sincere: Why should someone sell covered calls?
Trader: Covered call writing is an excellent strategy for investors who want to increase cash flow, that is, to provide a stream of income, but who recognize there is a limit to their upside profits. That limitation is difficult for some investors to overcome. Collecting the premium is the driving force for adopting this strategy. That means being assigned and selling the stock should be a very satisfying result.

Sincere: Is there any preparation needed before using this strategy?
Trader: If they already own the stock and know why they bought the stock, and want to continue to own the stock, then no, there's no preparation other than choosing an expiration date, strike price, and an acceptable premium. First, they must want this stock in their portfolio. Second, they must be certain the return on their investment—ROI—is acceptable.

Sincere: What's the major risk of using this strategy?
Trader: The major risk is the same for any person who owns stock, and that is the price can undergo a serious decline. An inconvenience occurs because you sold a call, thereby giving someone else the right to buy your stock. So, you must continue to own that stock until the option expires or until you repurchase the call. When your stock is above the strike price at expiration and the stock is called, that is not really a risk. That is achieving the maximum possible profit when adopting the covered call writing strategy.

Sincere: Does it bother you when the stock keeps rising higher and higher past the strike price?

Trader: No. I had the maximum potential profit in mind and that includes selling the stock at the strike price. It's similar to selling stock and then regretting a subsequent rally. If I knew which stocks were moving higher and lower, I'd be a billionaire. When I make my profit, I am never disappointed. I don't recommend the strategy if you're going to regret selling your stock.

Sincere: What should a covered call writer do if their stock is falling?

Trader: With a mental stop loss in place, investors should take the loss and get out. However, stocks do not often decline to that stop loss price. When they want to hold onto those shares, I recommend buying back the call option sold earlier and selling a new call with a new lower strike price and a further expiration date. It's called "rolling down the position." The additional premium collected represents a new source of income. It should not be looked upon as a way to "get back to even." It is a way to reduce your losses.

Sincere: What's the biggest mistake that covered call writers make?

Trader: They buy stock because the option premium is high just so they can collect a hefty premium. It looks like an attractive strategy. However, the option premium is high for a reason and that is because the stock price is volatile, giving the option buyer a chance to make some good money. When you get those high premiums, market participants believe there's an increased probability that the stock price will change significantly—perhaps due to an earnings announcement—and you'll incur a loss on the trade. Sure, an upside move is good for the covered call seller, but upside profits are capped and downside losses are not. Thus, if the stock price moves lower, it can be painful.

Sincere: How much profit do you aim to make on a trade?
Trader: Profits should be measured as a return on the investment, and not in a specific number of dollars. If I were to answer: "$300" to your question, that would tell you absolutely nothing. When writing an option with a potential return of 2.5% in one month, that's good in my opinion. I always calculated the potential profit by assuming the stock price remains unchanged. So, my 100 shares cost $10,000 and I collected $250 for the option. I would think of $250, or 2.5% of the investment, as the potential return. However, when the call option is out of the money, there is always a chance to earn more profit if the stock price were to be higher than my purchase price at expiration.

Sincere: How do you reduce risk when selling covered calls?
Trader: If reducing risk is a top priority, sell an option with a lower strike price. For example, if a stock is trading at $51 per share, instead of selling the 55 call, choose the 50 call instead. That brings in a higher premium, which translates into more protection against a loss, but it also increases the chances of being assigned and selling the stock.

Sincere: Why would you sell a $51 stock at the 50 strike? Some readers may think you'll have an immediate loss of $100.
Trader: The answer is you won't. If I collect a $300 premium, and later assigned, my profit would be $200. The net proceeds from the transaction would be $5,000 for the stock and $300 for the option. When the cost was $5,100 and the net proceeds for the sale is $5,300, that's a $200 profit.

Sincere: Do you have any other ideas to increase premium?
Trader: You can also sell an option with a longer expiration such as three or six months. As you know, the

longer the option lifetime, the greater the time premium in that option. A higher premium reduces any loss but it takes additional time to earn the premium, that is, more time is required for the option to expire. For patient investors who want extra downside protection, this is not a bad idea.

Sincere: Why don't you write out-of-the-money calls?
Trader: The reason is that I never pretend that I can predict stock market direction. Covered call writing is already a bullish position and I did not want to take an even more bullish stance. I wrote in-the-money calls with a satisfactory potential return on my investment. If I can earn 2% to 3% in one month, that's a pretty good annual return of 24% to 36%, ignoring compounding. When that possible profit comes with a couple of points of extra downside protection, I prefer that to giving up that protection and seeking a higher upside return. Most investors see only the bullish outcome and always sell OTM calls.

Sincere: What strike price should a beginner choose?
Trader: There is no good reply. There are no aspects of this strategy that are written in stone. You have your investment goals and risk tolerance, and so does every other trader. Plus, there is the psychological aspect that comes from feeling anguish over missing out on a sizable profit, or from losing a stock via assignment. There is no way to measure that anguish or to put a price tag on it. That being said, beginners should write an OTM call because it is easier to look at the trade as one that has a chance to make a good-sized profit, a relative term that varies for each trader.

Sincere: How about in-the-money calls? Should everyone write them?
Trader: Absolutely not. This is for investors who knowingly sacrifice upside potential for a better chance of exiting the

trade with a profit. Don't adopt this or any option strategy without a full understanding of how it works.

Sincere: Can you give a definition of what you mean by "downside protection"?
Trader: Downside protection is another way of describing the breakeven price for the covered call position when the stock price falls. It is the expiration stock price below which the trade loses money. Anything above that price results in a profit.

Sincere: How do you calculate that?
Trader: The calculation is easy. Determine the cost of the investment, which is the stock price minus the option premium, multiplied by the number of shares. If the stock is $47.50 and I sell an option at $4.00, I am protected against loss down to $43.50 (editor note: $4,750 - $400 / 100). If you don't write covered calls and just own the stock, you have no downside protection.

Sincere: How do you approach a covered call writing trade?
Trader: I view covered call writing as a business. I want to earn profits with acceptable risk. I don't think about where the stock price is expected to be in the future. I am not a good predictor. I have downside risk when buying stock. I chose a trade with a satisfactory upside profit potential that compensates me for the risk. I choose an expiration date based on the implied volatility of the option compared with the historical implied volatility for the options of this stock. Many of your readers may not be ready to learn about implied volatility, but I mention it for those who are.

Sincere: Is it a good outcome if an option expires worthless?

Trader: It depends. If the stock price has undergone a huge decline, then the answer is no. It is not a good outcome. But if the option is OTM by a very small amount at expiration, then that is a good outcome. Tell me my ROI for the trade, and then I will tell you whether the outcome is good.

Sincere: Is early assignment likely?
Trader: A call is almost never exercised before the expiration date because there is no reason for the option owner to take possession of the stock and inherit extra downside risk. The only exception occurs when exercising a call to collect a dividend. Risk lurks even here. Many dividends are too small to accept the risk of stock ownership.

Sincere: Should an investor close the call before the expiration date?
Trader: If the option can be bought at a low-enough price so that the vast majority of the profit potential has already been collected, then sure, do it. It depends on how much time is left. I wouldn't buy the option when expiration is only a few days down the road. When the remaining profit potential is down to $0.05, I tend to buy to close the position and immediately sell another call option with a later expiration date. In that scenario, there is no reason to wait for the option to expire.

Sincere: Why do some people try to avoid assignment?
Trader: Harsh as it may sound, it's probably because they have no idea what they are doing. When the investor truly changes their mind about selling the stock, and if they are willing to take a loss on the option by covering, then covering the short option is a reasonable thing to do. That would leave the investor owning the stock with no

remaining obligation to sell the shares. However, if the decision to cover the short option is the result of a rally in the stock price without a true desire to hold onto the shares, then covering the short option for the sole purpose of avoiding assignment is proof that this investor does not understand the risk-reward profile for writing covered calls.

Sincere: Are you saying that some covered call writers misunderstand the strategy?

Trader: Yes. The problem is that too many people truly lack an understanding of how covered call writing works. When the stock price rises, they panic, believing that they now hold a position fraught with risk, and that they are losing money. No money has been lost, unless you unwisely consider missing out on a possible profit as losing money. When I sold this call, I was willing to sell the stock at the strike price. I can't help it if the stock is above the strike, but it is a good thing for me because it is now more likely that I will earn the maximum possible profit for the covered call position. I do not understand why any trader would be displeased with this result. I'll accept assignment at expiration and move on to something else.

Sincere: Can you explain the importance of *time premium*?

Trader: The time premium represents the investor's profit potential. Sure, when the option is OTM, there is additional potential profit from an increase in the stock price, but the option profit is limited to its time premium. Remember that time premium is the portion of an option's price that the buyer pays for the possibility that the stock price will move favorably—higher for call options and lower for put options—thereby increasing the option premium and allowing the option to be sold at a profit. We, as option sellers, are not seeking a jump in the stock price—although it should be appreciated when it happens. We are collecting the premium instead of hoping for a stock price surge. And when selling OTM options, we do allow ourselves to go after some additional upside profits.

Sincere: How important is *intrinsic value*?
Trader: Remember, the price of an option is intrinsic value plus time premium. Intrinsic value is the amount that the option is in the money. In other words, how far above the call strike price the stock is trading. When a stock is $42 per share and the option price is $3.45, then the intrinsic value of a call with a 40-strike is $2.00 and the remaining portion of the option premium is the time premium, which is $1.45 in this example. Out-of-the-money options have no intrinsic value. So, how important is it? It is important when the trader wants to increase downside protection, but it plays zero role in determining the profit opportunity. Repeating what I said earlier: when selling a covered call option, it is the time premium that translates into profit potential, not the intrinsic value.

Sincere: Are the Greeks important to covered call writers?
Trader: Greeks are very important for advanced option traders. However, when your only strategy is writing covered calls, there is no reason to pay attention to the Greeks. Why? Because the Greeks are used to measure risk characteristics of any option position and we know that covered call selling is a bullish strategy. The only Greek of relevance for readers of this book is theta. Theta represents the amount by which the option price deteriorates in one day, assuming all other variables that affect an option's price remain unchanged.

BEYOND THE BASICS

I hope you gained new insights into how a professional trader sells covered calls. In the interview, you were introduced to a few new terms that are useful to option traders: *intrinsic value*, *time value* (or *time premium*), *historical volatility*, and *implied volatility*. These options concepts are important to learn, especially as you gain more experience. For starters, they help option traders calculate the profit potential for the trade.

To help understand these terms, the following sidebar should be useful. However, even after reading the sidebar, don't worry if you don't understand these concepts at first. With experience, it should make more sense. My suggestion is to re-read the interview and the sidebar after you've made a number of covered call transactions.

Intrinsic value, time value, historical volatility, and implied volatility

The following theoretical discussion is a little beyond the beginner level, but every options trader should learn these concepts eventually. Although you can sell covered calls without thoroughly understanding these ideas, knowing them will help make you a much stronger options trader.

Intrinsic value (for in-the-money options)

When you look at an option price, the portion of the premium that is in the money is its *intrinsic value*. To be precise, intrinsic value is the cash the option buyer would receive when they exercise the option and immediately sell the stock.

Put another way, intrinsic value is the difference between the current market stock price and the option's strike price. It's also the portion of the option that won't lose value because of the passage of time. In fact, intrinsic value is immune to the passage of time.

You already learned that an option's intrinsic value is the "in-the-money" portion of the option price. It is how much the stock price surpasses the strike price. Intrinsic value is never less than zero.

It's easy to calculate intrinsic value. For example, if Coca-Cola is $70 per share, then the intrinsic value of the 69 call is $1. It's simply the difference between the underlying stock price and the strike price.

Here's an example: If a stock is trading at $35 and the strike price is 33, the intrinsic value of the call option is $2. It has an intrinsic value of $2 regardless of the expiration date. (All options with a strike price equal to, or above the stock price, have zero intrinsic value.)

Note: It's the call option itself that has an intrinsic value but if and only if it's in the money. In other words, an in-the-money option has intrinsic value. It is worth something tangible.

Time value (or time premium)

Time value is simply what is left over after the intrinsic value is subtracted from the premium. For example, if the Coca-Cola call option costs $1.30 and the intrinsic value of the option is $1.00, then its time value is $.30 per share. The more time left until expiration, the greater the time value. During the last day before the market closes on expiration Friday, there is hardly any time value remaining.

The last 30 days of an option is when time value declines more rapidly. For example, if you track the value of a February option contract and compare it with one that expires in March or April, you will see that the February option loses value more rapidly.

This is one reason why options are called "wasting assets." Their value fades away as time passes. The rate that time value is lost is not linear (i.e., not a fixed amount every day). With a few exceptions, the rate of time decay increases each day until it disappears altogether.

Time value can vanish under two conditions: 1. Expiration has arrived. On the close of business on the expiration date, an option has no (zero) time value. 2. The option is so far out of the money that it is worthless.

Here's a formula that may help you understand time value:

Time value (or time premium) + intrinsic value = option premium

Volatility

To understand option pricing, it's essential to know the basics of *volatility*. At the most elementary level, a volatile stock will, on average, undergo daily price changes larger than those of less-volatile stocks. That is why their options trade with a higher premium. Call buyers must pay more for the options of volatile stocks because there is a good chance the option will gain value, and deliver a profit to its owner, before expiration.

Volatile stocks move by significant amounts in both directions, which is not good for anyone who

owns the shares, and that includes covered call sellers. If an investor is willing to accept the downside risk that comes with owning a volatile stock, then they will be happy to collect a very attractive price when writing a covered call.

Conversely, a really tame "Steady Eddie" stock may be a poor choice for covered call sellers because the premium is so low (although the same stock may be an excellent choice for buy-and-hold investors).

As mentioned earlier, more promising covered call prospects are "Steady Freddies," which are not too hot (too volatile) and not too cold (too tame). Steady Freddies are good covered call candidates because they are not too risky to own.

Note: You can find stocks that fit the above profiles by studying indexes such as the S&P 500 or the Dow Jones Industrial Average (DJIA). Start your research by creating a "Watch List" of potential covered call stock candidates.

Historical volatility

Historical volatility, displayed as a percentage, measures how much a stock has moved on a daily basis over a certain period in the past. For example, let's say that the average daily range for a $50 stock over the last six months is approximately $.10 (or 0.2 percent). The greater the daily percentage range of the stock price, the greater the volatility.

If a stock moves no more than 2 or 3 percent within six months or a year, it has a low historical volatility. A stock that moves 20 or 30 percent in a year has a higher historical volatility.

How does this help a covered call writer? Option prices are higher when the underlying stock is more volatile. Therefore, the higher the volatility, the higher the premium, but also the higher the probability the stock will make big moves in either direction.

Typically, option traders compare the historical volatility with what you will learn about next: *implied volatility*. Comparing the historical volatility of a stock with the implied volatility of its options helps option traders determine whether an option is over- or underpriced. (By the way, historical volatility for a stock can be found on your brokerage platform or on most financial websites.)

Implied volatility

When looking at option prices, there is a somewhat mysterious factor that helps to quantify how much an option is worth: *implied volatility*. Although not always easy for some people to understand, you should know that implied volatility is very important to option traders.

Implied volatility (IV), displayed as a percentage, is an estimate of how much the market expects the stock price to change over the lifetime of the option. When plugged into an option-pricing model, it is used by option traders to determine the theoretical (fair) value of an option contract. It is based on what the market believes (or implies) the option is worth.

Unlike historical volatility, which can be measured exactly, implied volatility is more like a real-time indicator of how much the market is willing to pay for the option. Using a calculator and the actual market price, we can calculate implied volatility.

Another way to think of implied volatility is the feeling of urgency that some traders have about options. Because of this urgency, you'll see higher IV on options that are in the greatest demand. Lots of buying pushes option prices higher. It's the urgency, or expectation, that the stock price might undergo a big change that drives traders to bid-up the options, forcing both the premium and the implied volatility higher.

Generally, stocks like Nvidia and Google had very high implied volatility—and might today. You can sense the urgency to own options before an earnings release or some other important news announcement. Guess what? Nvidia options were expensive because of its high implied volatility. Conversely, the lack of urgency of options on stocks such as Johnson & Johnson typically means there is no urgency, and no pressure on the premium. Therefore, the IV doesn't increase. For stocks whose options have low implied volatility, option prices are lower. There isn't the same demand for these options, nor is there any expectation that the stock price will change significantly.

Market makers always know the implied volatility

because their computers generate that number based on all the factors that go into pricing an option. The market makers set the original option prices, but at times, supply and demand force them to raise and lower prices.

Therefore, if the implied volatility of a call or put is too high, then the option would be viewed as over-priced. Option buyers end up paying much more than the option is worth.

Implied volatility is useful to covered call sellers because the higher the IV, the higher the premium received when writing a call option, and the greater the potential profits. To increase profit potential, covered call sellers will look for options with higher IV (but not too high). Also, be aware that options with higher IV will sometimes have a wider bid-ask spread.

Bottom line: Knowing what an option is worth provides a big edge. In the end, however, it's the market that determines the true value of an option. Unfortunately, sometimes it's only after the fact that we know whether an option was over- or underpriced.

Many option traders don't understand implied volatility, but it's worth the effort to study and learn, especially as you gain more experience. Implied volatility is especially important to option speculators.

Note: Your brokerage firm has software that gives the implied volatility of options. This software is based on the once-revolutionary options pricing model, *Black-Scholes or Cox-Ross-Rubenstein.*

> Note: One reason many people lose money speculating with options is they don't understand option pricing. They shouldn't blame options for their lost money. They should blame themselves for trading far too early in their education process.

CONCLUSION

I hope you found the discussion with an experienced, professional trader useful. As I wrote earlier, it may be helpful to re-read this chapter after you've gained more experience and have a better understanding of how this strategy works.

In the next chapter, we will return to basics. I will show you the steps to take when applying for a Level 1 options trading account. If you already have permission to sell covered calls, feel free to skip to the Closing Comments, the last chapter of the book.

CHAPTER 9

HOW TO APPLY FOR AN OPTIONS ACCOUNT

If you are excited about selling covered calls but haven't yet opened an account, this chapter is for you. In fact, one of my goals for writing this book was to not only teach you how to sell covered calls, but to motivate you to do so.

I learned from experience that a lot of people want to read about options but are nervous or unsure about opening a real account and trading with real money. In this short chapter, I guide you through the few necessary steps. As you will discover, the approval process for selling covered calls is very straightforward.

HOW TO GET APPROVED FOR OPTION TRADING

Many of you may have a brokerage account where you can trade stocks, and that's great. To sell covered calls, however, you must ask your brokerage for permission to trade options. It's easiest to apply online or use an app. More than likely, you will be approved quickly, especially after reading this book.

After opening a brokerage account and getting approved for option trading, you now have an opportunity to make more money.

Note: If you do not have a stock brokerage account, the following sidebar tells you how to open one. (Skip the sidebar if you already have a brokerage account.)

How to open a stock brokerage account

Before you can trade stocks or options, the first action is to open an account at a brokerage firm, a company licensed to buy and sell stocks, options, and other financial products on behalf of its clients (such as you). The broker acts as a middleman between you and other buyers and sellers.

It's important to choose a firm with a good reputation, low fees, and an online help desk, in case you have questions. To find a reputable brokerage, type "find top-rated brokerage firms," followed by the current year into a search engine. A list of top-rated brokerage firms will be displayed from the websites of reputable, independent news sources such as *Forbes*, *Barron's*, MarketWatch, *Kiplinger*, *USA Today*, NerdWallet, and Bankrate, to name a few.

Before signing with a broker, get a copy of their fee schedule for stocks and option contracts. It shouldn't cost much, perhaps $.50 to $.65 for each option contract. However, you don't want a brokerage firm that overcharges on each options contract (like they did in the old days).

Find out the brokerage firm's requirements for selling covered calls. Be certain that you ask about *covered calls*. Nearly every brokerage firm allows covered writing, a Level 1 options strategy. Call, email, or chat with the representatives to make sure before opening the account.

After choosing a broker, opening the account is as simple as opening a checking or savings account. Fill out a questionnaire and provide your social security number and date of birth.

There is no need to fund the account right away (i.e., deposit money). All you have to do is open the account online or with an app, or visit the brokerage office (if they have one). However, you must fund the account prior to submitting an order for any stock or option trade.

Permission to sell covered calls

On the questionnaire, you will be asked basic questions about your investment experience, your financial objectives, the products you want to own (such as stocks or options), and the risk you are willing to take (from low to high).

Don't worry too much about the answers to the questionnaire, but do mention that you are willing to take some risk.

One question on the form asks whether you want to trade options. Answer YES. When asked what option strategies you want to use, only mention covered calls (a Level 1 strategy). Because you read this book, you should have no problem answering the questions.

The margin account

If you are selling covered calls, you do NOT need a margin account (although some strategies require that you have one). For beginners, I recommend not applying for margin as it can cause future problems.

Once you receive permission to trade covered calls, there are only a couple more steps.

1. Sign the options agreement and questionnaire

To trade options, you must fill out an options agreement from your brokerage. The purpose of the agreement is to determine your level of knowledge and experience, and also to find out how much risk you are willing to take. As you already know, selling covered calls is one of the most conservative option strategies. The odds are very good you will be approved.

2. Read the Options Disclosure Document (ODD)

After signing up for option trading, the broker is also required to give you a lengthy, technical document, *Characteristics and Risks of Standardized Options*, which you can download.

Written by lawyers, the document explains the different ways to lose money when trading options, including every possible risk. Because you read Chapter 7, you are already aware of the risks pertaining to covered calls.

In the document, you will read that "an option is the right to buy or sell a specified amount or value of a particular underlying interest at a fixed exercise price by exercising the option before its specified expiration date." The fixed exercise price is the strike price.

You will also read that the seller (writer) of a covered call becomes obligated to sell the underlying security to the buyer at the strike price if the option is exercised.

The most important part is this: Options are legal contracts that give their owner certain rights, and the sellers have certain obligations. With any call option, the buyer has the *right* to buy the underlying stock at a predetermined price (the strike price).

Conversely, the seller (or writer) has the *obligation* to deliver (sell) those shares to the buyer at the strike price if the option is exercised. In exchange for this obligation, the option seller receives the premium upfront.

The OCC, and your broker, must be sure you're aware of all the potential risks. That is why they insist that all option traders read this intimidating document. Since you read this book, you already know most of the benefits and risks, as well as how to use this strategy.

YOU ARE APPROVED!

Congratulations! After getting approved, you may sell covered calls in your brokerage account. With the knowledge gained about options, I am confident that you will have few problems getting started. After that, the real learning begins.

As you know, the more you do something, the easier it becomes. Therefore, the more covered call trades made, the more knowledgeable and skilled you become.

Note: Although you may be allowed to sell covered calls in an IRA, I discourage it, at least until you gain a *lot* more experience. Some may want to speak to a financial advisor or tax accountant for guidance, and that's always a good idea. Like any tool, in the hands of an experienced investor, selling covered calls can enhance your returns. However, if you don't understand what you're doing, selling covered calls in a retirement account increases the risk that it will end badly. The last thing you want to do is put your retirement funds at risk.

CONCLUSION

It may be hard to believe but you completed the book. Well done! All that is left are a few closing comments and reference material. You are now ready to start making money by selling covered calls on the stocks you own.

Closing Comments

I have great news—you are now ready to sell covered calls!

As I wrote several times, I strongly suggest starting small. Even if you don't make a lot of money at first, starting small allows you to learn the nuances of the strategy without placing too much money at risk.

As you gain experience, you may increase the investment size, and the number of options contracts sold. Over time, you will find the type of stocks that you want to own for your covered call portfolio. In reality, sometimes even the best stocks go in the wrong direction, but as you gain more experience and skills, you'll know what to do.

More than likely, some of you may want to try more advanced option strategies, and that's fine. Just remember that the more speculative strategies are for the most experienced and knowledgeable traders. Once again, before jumping to advanced strategies, be certain you understand how to sell covered calls.

Selling covered calls is a wonderful way to make money, and with very little stress. As long as you pick desirable stocks, this strategy is a low-risk way to boost income.

Buy index funds (ETFs or mutual funds)

As mentioned earlier, in addition to using covered calls to boost your income, it's a good idea to have a core investment account, typically in an S&P 500 index fund, either as an ETF or mutual fund. Each month, invest a set sum into the index fund, a strategy called *dollar-cost averaging*.

Note: To read more about how to build wealth with index funds and stocks, I recommend a book I wrote: *Help Your Child Build Wealth* (Wiley, 2024).

After you've gained more experience

After you've gained more experience with options, some of you may want to read my follow-up book, the bestselling *Understanding Options* (McGraw Hill), which not only introduces the covered call strategy but also speculative strategies such as buying and selling calls and puts, spreads, and advanced option strategies. This book is not for everyone, but only for those who want to learn even more about options.

My own experience with options

I wrote this book to help other investors and traders avoid the mistakes that I made when first trading options. Of all the strategies, selling covered calls was not only the easiest to learn, but increased my income every few months. I also experimented with some of the more speculative option strategies and although I had some initial success, making consistent profits was elusive.

To earn profits speculating with options, you must be right about the underlying stock, the direction, and most importantly, the timing. Although I had many good days, in the end it became too risky for me. For my personality, I learned that selling covered call options was much better than placing a bet on the future direction of stocks that I did not own.

Although selling covered calls is a slower way to make money, it is an easier and more consistent path to increasing cash flow. If you follow the suggestions in this book, you'll rarely have to worry that you'll lose a large sum because the stock you choose plunged.

Advanced option strategies

One day, you may run into option traders who will try to convince you to use more advanced strategies, some with sexy names such as the *iron condor*, the *butterfly*, *calendar spreads*, and *straddles*. They will claim that you can make a lot more money with these more advanced strategies than with selling covered calls.

Theoretically, they are right. Unfortunately, the more speculative strategies come with a lot more risk. And worse, it takes a lot more skill to use these sophisticated strategies. That's one reason I urge people to spend at least a year learning the covered call strategy.

Then, and only then, can you even think about speculating. Based on my own experience, research, and interviews with dozens of experts, being a long-term investor in addition to selling covered calls makes the most sense.

In reality, every person is different. Some may find selling covered calls too limiting, and will gravitate towards option strategies that come with the chance to earn more money. That is their choice. But to the majority of beginners, I say stick with the so-called simple strategy of selling or writing covered calls.

IT'S TIME TO SAY GOODBYE

As an author, it is gratifying to know that you took the time to buy and read my book. In return, I hope it met your needs and expectations. If it did, I'm be happy for you. I also hope that with the information you learned from this book, it helps you to increase income with covered calls.

Some of you may want to re-read certain chapters in the future as a refresher course, and that's not a bad idea. You have absorbed a ton of information, and some of it will be forgotten.

If you have questions about anything you read in this book, feel free to email me, Mr. Sincere, at my email address: **msincere@gmail.com**. Also, if you notice any errors, please let me know so I can make corrections in the next printing.

RESOURCES

As mentioned earlier, the best source for options information is the OIC, the educational arm of the OCC. They will answer any option question Monday through Friday, and probably respond within the same day. You can email the OIC at this email address: options@theocc.com.

In addition to the OIC, consider looking at the following websites and apps for additional information about stocks and options. Those organizations preceded by an asterisk (*) are accessible through a paid subscription.

*AAII: http://www.aaii.com

Bankrate: http://www.bankrate.com

Barchart: http://www.barchart.com

**Barron's*: http://www.barrons.com

Benzinga: http://www.benzinga.com

Bloomberg: http://www.bloomberg.com

Briefing: http://www.briefing.com

CBOE: www.cboe.com

CNBC: http://www.cnbc.com

CNN Business: http://Money.cnn.com

**Financial Times*: http://www.ft.com

Forbes: http://www.forbes.com

Fox Business News: http://www.foxbusiness.com

Google Finance: http://www.google.com/finance

Investopedia: http://www.investopedia.com
*_Investor's Business Daily_: http://www.investors.com
*Kiplinger: http://www.kiplinger.com
MarketWatch: http://www.marketwatch.com
The MoneyShow: http://www.moneyshow.com
Morningstar: http://www.morningstar.com
The Motley Fool: http://www.fool.com
MSN Money: http://www.msn.com
Nasdaq: http://www.nasdaq.com
New York Stock Exchange: http://www.nyse.com
NerdWallet: http://www.nerdwallet.com
OCC: http://www.theocc.com
OIC: http://www.optionseducation.org
Real Clear Markets: http://www.realclearmarkets.com
SEC: http://www.sec.gov
Seeking Alpha: http://www.seekingalpha.com
StockCharts: http://www.stockcharts.com
*The Street: http://www.thestreet.com
TradingView: http://www.tradingview.com
*Value Line: http://www.valueline.com
*_Wall Street Journal_: http://www.wsj.com
Wikiinvest: http://www.wikiinvest.com
Yahoo Finance: http://finance.yahoo.com
*Zacks Investment Research: http://www.zacks.com

About the Author

Mr. Sincere is a freelance writer and author who writes easy-to-understand articles, columns and books about investing and trading. He's an expert at helping readers of all ages understand complicated financial topics.

Some of his books include *Understanding Stocks* (McGraw Hill) and *Understanding Options* (McGraw Hill), each which sold over 100,000 copies. He also wrote an investment book for parents and older teenagers: *Help Your Child Build Wealth: A Parent's Guide to Teaching Children to Be Successful Investors* (Wiley, 2024).

Mr. Sincere has been interviewed on dozens of national radio programs and has appeared on financial news TV programs such as CNBC and ABC's *World News Now* to talk about his books.

When Mr. Sincere is not writing, he's riding one of his e-bikes, or traveling, or doing both. If you have questions or comments, write him at msincere@gmail.com. You can also visit his website and read his blog at www.michaelsincere.com.

www.ingramcontent.com/pod-product-compliance
Lightning Source LLC
LaVergne TN
LVHW090417210926
848480LV00002B/594

* 9 7 9 8 9 9 2 3 6 4 7 2 9 *